STRATEGIES FOR PROJECT SPONSORSHIP

STRATEGIES FOR PROJECT SPONSORSHIP

Vicki James
Ron Rosenhead
Peter Taylor

MANAGEMENTCONCEPTSPRESS

MANAGEMENTCONCEPTS PRESS
8230 Leesburg Pike, Suite 800
Tysons Corner, VA 22182
(703) 790-9595
Fax: (703) 790-1371
www.managementconcepts.com

Copyright © 2013 by Management Concepts, Inc.

All rights reserved. No part of this book may be reproduced or utilized in any form or by any means, electronic or mechanical, including photocopying, recording, or by an information storage and retrieval system, without permission in writing from the authors and the publisher, except for brief quotations in review articles.

Library of Congress ECPN Data: 2013933648

ISBN 978-1-56726-406-7

Printed in the United States of America

About the Authors

Vicki James is passionate about learning and sharing best practices in project management and business analysis. Certified in both project management (Project Management Professional® certification from the Project Management Institute since 2005) and business analysis (Certified Business Analysis Professional from the International Institute of Business Analysis since 2010), she provides a broad view to support project governance and processes.

Vicki spent 11 years in the public sector successfully delivering projects to support governmental operations. Today she provides private training and consulting to government and private industry clients in addition to writing and presenting on all things project. She also serves as president of the International Institute of Business Analysis (IIBA, Seattle Chapter, 2012–2014).

Vicki was a contributor to *The Complete Project Manager* (2012) by Randall Englund and Alfonso Bucero and is a popular blogger and tweeter. You can find more information to connect with or follow Vicki at www.project-pro.us.

Ron Rosenhead is known for his highly practical approach to project management. He has spent more than 25 years as a trainer and consultant; for the last 17 years he has specialized in helping organizations increase the probability of project success. He has personally trained and coached over 10,000 people in the project management world, including both project managers and project sponsors, across all sectors.

He is also a professional speaker and author of *Deliver that Project* (ebook), as well as a regular blogger and tweeter. Ron writes practical project management training materials and has contributed to *Construction Stakeholder Management* (Wiley-Blackwell) and *Business Proficiency* (Klett International).

More information can be found at www.ronrosenhead.co.uk, www.projectagency.co.uk, and www.deliverthatproject.com. Ron can be contacted at rr@projectagency.com.

Peter Taylor is a dynamic and commercially astute professional who has achieved notable success in project management.

He has 27 years of experience in project management and marketing and has spent the last eight years leading program management offices (PMOs) and developing project managers. He is now an independent PMO coach, workshop trainer and consultant, and professional speaker, as well as the author of *The Lazy Project Manager* (Infinite Ideas), *The Lazy Project Manager and the Project from Hell* (Infinite Ideas), *Leading Successful PMOs* (Gower), *The Lazy Winner* (Infinite Ideas), and *Project Branding* (RMC, June 2013).

More information about Peter's work can be found at www.thelazyprojectmanager.com, www.leadingsuccessfulpmos.com, and www.thelazywinner.com, and through his free podcasts in iTunes. If you would like to learn even more, Peter can be contacted for articles, training, workshops, presentations, and keynotes at peter.b.taylor@btinternet.com.

Dedicated to all the project sponsors who contributed to this book by delivering the projects that have shaped our knowledge of what "good sponsorship" is.

Contents

Foreword xiii
Preface xix
Acknowledgments xxiii

Introduction to Project Sponsorship 1
What Is Project Sponsorship? 2
The Sponsor's Role 5
What Do the Professionals Say? 9
Who Does What and When? 10

Part I   For the Project Manager 15

Chapter 1   Preparing to Work with Your Sponsor 17
Who Should Sponsor Your Project? 18
Assessing Your Sponsor 19
Interviewing the Sponsor 25
Kicking Off Your Relationship with the Sponsor 30

Chapter 2   Working with a Sponsor 47
Using Your Influence 48
Asking Your Sponsor for Help 52
Giving Feedback to Your Sponsor 53
Delivering Bad News 57
Coaching Your Sponsor 60
The Sponsor Responsibilities Evaluation Tool 61

Sharing the Project Passion with Your Sponsor 66
Planning for a Sponsor's Sudden Absence 67
The Project Manager Evaluation Tool 69

Chapter 3   Working with Challenging Sponsors 73
The Absent Sponsor 75
The Busy Sponsor...79
The Uninterested Sponsor 81
The Inexperienced Sponsor...83
The Sponsor Who Wants to Be the Project Manager 84
The Sponsor Who Gets Involved Too Late 87
The Untrained Sponsor 89
The Sponsor Who Is Part of a Committee of Sponsors 91
The Saboteur or Just Plain Bad Sponsor...94
When All Else Fails 97
The Now and Wow Factor..99

Chapter 4   Managing Your Project's Stakeholders 103
Stakeholder Identification...104
Stakeholder Analysis...104
Stakeholder Engagement 107
The Influence Map 108

Part II   For the Sponsor..117

Chapter 5   Sponsoring Your First Project.....................................119
Stories from the Strategies for Project Sponsorship Survey 119
The Accidental Project Sponsor 123
Transitioning from Project Manager to Sponsor 124
Taking Sponsorship Seriously 126

Chapter 6   Sponsor Responsibilities and Best Practices 131
Providing Direction and Guidance Strategies and Initiatives 132
Working with the Project Manager to Develop the Project Charter.........133
Identifying and Quantifying Business Benefits to Be Achieved 133

Making Go/No-Go Decisions 135
Evaluating the Project's Success Upon Completion...................137
Negotiating Funding for the Project..138
Actively Participating in Initial Project Planning 139
Reviewing and Approving Changes to Plans, Priorities, Deliverables,
    Schedule, and More..139
Identifying Project Steering Committee Members 140
Chairing the Project Steering Committee 141
Assisting the Project When Required..141
Assisting with the Resolution of Interproject Boundary Issues 142
Supporting the Project Manager in Conflict Resolution 142
Making the Project Visible Within the Organization................142
Encouraging Stakeholder Involvement and Building and
    Maintaining Ongoing Commitment 143
Advising the Project Manager About Protocols, Political Issues,
    and Potential Sensitivities 144

Part III   **For the Organization** 147

Chapter 7   **Developing the Sponsor** 149
Too Cool for School: Making Sponsorship Training Work 149
Fifty Secrets to Being a Good Project Sponsor 153
Developing Your Organization's Sponsorship Capability 160
Categorizing Projects and Selecting Sponsors 162
Can Your Project Management Office Help? 164

Afterword.. 171

Appendix A   **Sponsorship Survey Results** 177

Appendix B   **The Definitive Project Sponsor Checklist** 189

Appendix C   **The Definitive Project Manager Checklist** 191

Appendix D   **The 50 Secrets to Being a Good Executive
    Sponsor** 193

Appendix E   Additional Resources on Project Sponsorship..........197

Index...199

Foreword

There is an old saying that we can pick our friends but not our relatives. Similarly, a project manager can often pick his or her team but rarely, if ever, the executive sponsor. Yet, projects cannot succeed without an engaged and skillful executive sponsor or project owner.

Strategies for Project Sponsorship offers project managers, project sponsors, and executives insight into the key role of the sponsor. The authors have correctly identified that much has been done—and continues to be done—to develop the role of the project manager, but they have also identified that the role of the project sponsor has been sadly neglected to date—something the authors want to correct.

The Standish Group's CHAOS research, an ongoing survey of software development projects and their resolutions initiated in 1994 that is very well known in the project management community, has shown improvement in project outcomes—improvement that arguably can be perceived as excruciatingly slow. The study has also shown that the role of the executive sponsor is a critical success factor.

The authors focus on the executive sponsor and the sponsor's relationship with the project manager, because if the sponsor is critical to the successful outcome of any project, then so is the partnership of the sponsor and the project manager. In The Standish Group's survey, chief information officers (CIOs) said that it was important that the project manager bond with the executive sponsor; 43 percent said it was very important. A good example of the importance of this bond is a project undertaken by one of The Standish Group's clients, a large insurance company in the northwestern United States. The organization needed to replace its outdated general ledger application because it did not support the compliance requirements of Sarbanes-Oxley. In this case, the executive sponsor of the replacement project was the chief financial officer (CFO).

This CFO, like many of the CIOs we surveyed, thought it was important for the project manager and the executive sponsor to be on the same page in creating and maintaining the vision, objectives, and problem statements. She decided she wanted a project manager who understood the application package. The CFO directed the project management office (PMO) to find her a project manager with these skills. The PMO interviewed a number of external and internal project managers. They selected a couple of candidates and arranged a meeting with the CFO. The CFO met with the candidates and selected the one with whom she felt a bond, and with whom she felt she could establish a working relationship. Throughout the duration of the general ledger project, the executive sponsor and her handpicked project manager enjoyed a good working relationship that brought the project to completion early and under budget. This situation shows what is possible with a good bond between manager and sponsor. Therefore, if you work on your bond, you too can have this success.

Leadership and managing expectations of the executive sponsor are two of the most important skills that project managers need to master and continually improve. However, these skills are some of the most difficult to learn. The project manager will need to adopt a "servant leadership" style with the executive sponsor: to listen very carefully and reflectively, to empathize, to be aware of the sponsor's skills, and to rise above the sponsor's shortcomings.

The authors offer checklists for both the project manager and the executive sponsor to use in assessing themselves and each other, along with other diagnostic tools. The knowledge gained from these may go a long way toward helping the sponsor and the project manager work together to maximize each other's strengths, support each other's weaknesses, and build the trusting relationship that should be their goal.

Collaboration between the executive sponsor and the project manager is essential for the success of the project. However, creating the basis for this collaboration is not an easy task for the project manager, since the executive sponsor is usually at a much higher level within the organization. The project manager needs to take time and learn skills to create such a bond. Ninety-one percent of CIOs said that mastering the skill of bonding with the executive sponsor is difficult and reported that only 12 percent of their project managers are highly skilled at bonding with the executive sponsor. This book offers insights into the nature of building that relationship through the use of tools such as the power grid, influence mapping, and checklists, and it includes examples of dealing with specific types of challenging sponsors.

The authors bring good news in that executive sponsor bonding skills can be acquired and improved. Project managers can learn to communicate, negotiate, and build consensus with their executive sponsors, and they can learn to make sure that the project team, stakeholders, and other executives are on the same page as the executive sponsor. They can become skilled at working with the executive sponsor on general project optimization and financial controls. And they can discover how to work with the executive sponsor on presenting and dealing with bad news and difficult challenges.

Strategies for Project Sponsorship is a resource that project managers can use to master and hone their skills in bonding with the executive sponsor as well as a resource for would-be and current sponsors interested in assessing their strengths and weaknesses.

—Harry Stefanou, PhD
Retired Vice President, Global Alliances
Project Management Institute

—James Johnson
Chairman
The Standish Group

The longest word in the English language is the one that follows "And now a word from our sponsor..."

Preface

Whatever you may wish for as a project manager, the reality is that you have to work with the project sponsor you are given. This book offers project managers a range of practical techniques to get the best out of their project sponsors. It also demonstrates the value a good sponsor brings to projects and to the businesses she serves.

From the project sponsor's point of view, dealing with projects and project managers is not always easy. Often—very often—project sponsors will have received no training or support for their critical role. This book lays out clearly and straightforwardly what it means to be a good sponsor and how to work efficiently and effectively with a project manager.

Many speak of the "accidental project manager," but the reality is that the current generation of project sponsors can also be considered accidental project sponsors. Although they may not have any background in project management or project-based activity, having reached a senior level within their organization based on other achievements, they have assumed that role. Remember that there is not currently an official body of knowledge for project sponsors to help them understand best project management practices.

And finally, these days more than ever before, the projects that executives commission are critical to the strategic growth of organizations; those executives demand and expect the highest level of success. This book explores the important part that project sponsors can and should play in project success and why executives need to take the sponsorship community within their organizations to the next level by investing in support, development, and guidance.

Strategies for Project Sponsorship is based on research across all three communities: project managers, project sponsors, and executives. We are experienced project managers who know firsthand not only what it means to work with project sponsors but also to be a project sponsor working with project managers. Through our own experience and research in project management, we have identified a gap in the focus of effort in the area of project sponsorship. Much has been done, and continues to be done, within project management, but the key role of project sponsor has been sadly neglected to date.

The Standish Group,[1] in its report *Chaos Manifesto 2012: The Year of The Executive Sponsor*, stated:

> We believe improvement in the skills of the executive sponsor is the single most important factor that will increase project success. Sixty-six percent of executive sponsors do a poor job and shirk their responsibilities. However, it is not their fault, because no one has educated them about their roles and responsibilities.[2]

Strategies for Project Sponsorship explores the challenges of working with and being a project sponsor from the various viewpoints of project managers, project sponsors, and organizations undertaking project-based activity to support their strategic visions.

The book provides examples from real-world experiences, as well as tips, techniques, and tools to help you get the most out of your project sponsor (or the project manager for whom you are serving as project sponsor). We begin by defining good project sponsorship and considering roles and responsibilities—who does what and when.

We then turn to the project manager's view: how to understand the project sponsor you have, how to work most effectively with project sponsors with different approaches and styles, how to develop the right relationship between the sponsor and the project manager, and what roles each should undertake. We also expand the discussion of sponsor management techniques to all stakeholders.

For the project sponsor, we address how to become a sponsor in the first place, how you may have "accidentally" assumed the role of sponsor, how to enhance your skills to become the best sponsor you can be, and what key duties a project sponsor should assume.

And finally, from the organization's point of view, we discuss how executives should encourage and support the sponsors within their organizations, and why should they consider project sponsorship advantageous to their business strategy.

Throughout this book we provide tools and guides that we hope are readily useful and of practical value to you in your project management and sponsorship work. If you have some ideas to add to this list or ways to improve on what we suggest, we encourage you to contact us at www.strategies4sponsors.com and share your experiences.

—Vicki James
—Ron Rosenhead
—Peter Taylor

NOTES

1 The reader will find many references to The Standish Group's 2012 CHAOS report, *The Year of the Executive Sponsor*, throughout this book. We would like to thank The Standish Group and Jim Johnson for sharing their research findings and their report with us. It has helped to provide an even better sense of the state of project sponsorship today and the strategies for industry improvements into the future. The Standish Group is based in Boston, Massachusetts, and is the IT leader in project and value performance. They are a group of highly dedicated professionals with years of practical experience in assessing risk, cost, return, and value for IT investments. The Standish Group provides IT investment planning research and services such as project assessments, requirements optimization, total cost of ownership, return on investment, risk analysis, and value analysis based on years of high-quality, independent primary research.
2 The Standish Group, *Chaos Manifesto 2012: The Year of the Executive Sponsor* (Boston: The Standish Group, 2012), 3.

Acknowledgments

Vicki thanks her coauthors: Peter, for taking a chance on this collaboration with an unpublished author, and Ron, for his attention to detail and plans that helped to keep the project on track. She would also like to thank Chandra Moss for inadvertently pushing her to achieve the PMP, the first step that sparked the passion for project management best practices that she has today. She also thanks Randy Englund and Alfonso Bucero for their book *Project Sponsorship: Achieving Management Commitment for Project Success*, which kicked off her interest in this topic and for the friendship that has since formed. And finally, she thanks Megan Pilon (project management office manager) and Lynne McGuire (sponsor of many projects), who were there in the early days of her career and helped shape the project manager she has become.

Ron thanks his fellow authors for their challenging approach and sense of humor. His wife Sue must also come in for special mention for helping to make the task of writing the book less daunting and much more enjoyable. He would also like to thank the many unnamed project sponsors he has met who have inspired him to create and develop, along with his fellow authors, this book.

Peter thanks his coauthors for their shared wisdom and experience, Sheilina Somani for the "good project sponsor" story (and the lunch), Eileen Roden for her roundtable inspiration at the APMG-International event in London, and Sarah Coleman for her insight. He also wishes to add his gratitude for the support from Jim Johnson of The Standish Group for sharing the work that they were undertaking with regard to executive sponsorship.

All the authors wish to thank everyone who contributed to this book by way of completing the survey, sharing their own sponsor story, joining in the Project Sponsors group discussions on LinkedIn, or reviewing the manuscript.

And thank you to Management Concepts for sponsoring the whole project.

If I had an hour to save the world, I would spend 59 minutes defining the problem and one minute finding solutions.

—Albert Einstein

Introduction to Project Sponsorship

All over the world, there has been much focus on the training and development of project managers. The growth in qualifications in this area has been immense and is matched by the growth in capability for the majority of project managers. But the lack of maturity of the project sponsor role and the lack of understanding of its importance leave a gap in project management. Our intent is to correct this gap.

Project sponsorship can be many things to many people. Sponsors, especially, may see their role differently from the way project managers perceive it. Sponsorship includes many senses of the word *sponsor* without a common understanding of the roles and responsibilities *to sponsor* across project industries.

Professionals may be unclear on a definition of the term, but project management practice gives us some idea of what a sponsor does, as distinct from a project manager, and why it is so important to the success of a project and to an organization's goals.

WHAT IS PROJECT SPONSORSHIP?

The *Oxford English Dictionary* offers many definitions for the word *sponsor*. Used as a noun, it can mean any of the following:

- A person or organization that pays for or contributes to the costs involved in staging a sporting or artistic event in return for advertising: *the production cost $80,000, most coming from local sponsors.*

- A person who pledges to donate a certain amount of money to another person after participating in a fundraising event organized on behalf of a charity.

- A person who introduces and supports a proposal for legislation: *a leading sponsor of the bill.*

- A person taking official responsibility for the actions of another: *they act as sponsors and contacts for new immigrants.*

- A person presenting a candidate for confirmation or baptism: Lisa has asked me to be her sponsor for confirmation next month.

The word can also be used as a verb, meaning

- To provide funds for (a project or activity or the person carrying it out): *Joe is being sponsored by a government training program.*

- To pay some or all of the costs involved in staging (a sporting or artistic event) in return for advertising: *the event is sponsored by Qantas Airlines.*

- To pledge to donate money on behalf of a participant in a fundraising event: *Nigella wishes to thank all those people who sponsored her.*

- To introduce and support a proposal in a legislative assembly: *the senator sponsored the bill.*

- To propose and organize negotiations or talks between other people or groups: *the U.S. sponsored negotiations between the two sides.*

Interestingly, even though the word *sponsor* has many meanings, there is no dictionary definition that in any way relates to project management and the topic of this book, project sponsorship. So given the lack of an authoritative definition of a project sponsor and the paucity of published writing about the role of project sponsorship, let's take a look at how one of the major project management professional certification bodies defines it. According to the Project Management Institute's (PMI's) *A Guide to the Project Management Body of Knowledge*[1] *(PMBOK® Guide)*:

> A sponsor is the person or group who provides resources and support for the project and is accountable for enabling success. The sponsor may be external or internal to the project manager's organization. From initial conception through project closure, the sponsor promotes the project. This includes serving as spokesperson to higher levels of management to gather support throughout the organization and promoting the benefits the project brings. The sponsor leads the project through the initiating processes until formally authorized, and plays a significant role in the development of the initial scope and charter. For issues that are beyond control of the project manager, the sponsor serves as an escalation path. The sponsor may also be involved in other important issues such as authorizing changes in scope, phase-end reviews, and go/no-go decisions when risks are particularly high. The sponsor also ensures a smooth transfer of the project's deliverables into the business of the requesting organization after project closure.[2]

Considering this definition and applying our own observations from experience, discussions, and surveys, we can surmise that a project sponsor is the person in an organization who will

- Realize the most benefit to business value from the project
- Actively seek or provide funding to support the project
- Set the parameters and expectations for project success
- Provide high-level monitoring of the project to ensure the expected value will be realized
- Promote the project to ensure visibility and increase the chance for success
- Actively be involved in risk identification, management, and mitigation
- Authorize significant project changes to extend or compress scope, schedule, budget, or quality.

In short, this high-level list shows that the project sponsor is the person in the organization who most cares about the project and its success. At least she should be.

Take a look at Figure I-1. Every project begins with an idea. The business case, based on that idea, explains the project and its expected benefits. The sponsor must believe in the project and in the anticipated benefits. She will bring the project to the portfolio committee or other authority within the organization responsible for providing funding. This committee provides funding to the sponsor, with the condition that the sponsor will provide the executive-level project oversight. Now the project can begin. The first steps include selecting a project manager and developing a project charter or other initiating document.

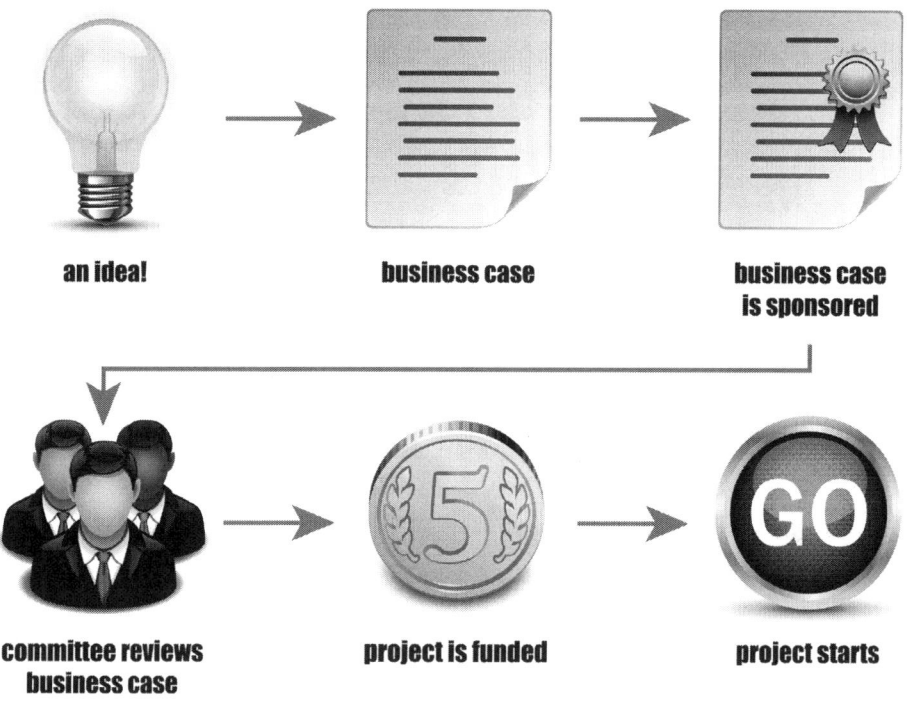

FIGURE I-1: Simplified Project Sponsorship Process

Figure I-1 illustrates just one common example of how projects come to be. There are as many different variations as there are organizations in the world. One common thread in most projects is that the sponsor is given funding with the expectation that she will have executive oversight and responsibility for the project.

THE SPONSOR'S ROLE

Project sponsorship is an active senior management role. A sponsor is responsible for identifying the business need, problem, or opportunity. Once this has been done, the sponsor ensures the project remains a viable proposition and that the expected business benefits are realized. During project performance, the sponsor focuses on resolving any issues outside the control of the project manager and acting as the project's champion.

The role of sponsor is a far-reaching one. It can't be considered a full-time role—unlike the role of the project manager for a significant project—but it does require a depth of knowledge, experience in project activity, a power base of some influence, and an alert and decisive mind.

A project sponsor is not a sponsor for life—that is, she has other roles and responsibilities that don't pertain to the project—but she is there for the duration of the project, from initiation to closure. Randy Englund and Alfonso Bucero write

> A good sponsor performs different functions during the project life cycle, serving as mentor, catalyst, motivator, barrier buster, and boundary manager. The sponsor is the link between the project manager and senior managers. The project sponsor is the best "project seller." The sponsor promotes and defends the project in front of all other stakeholders. Being a project sponsor is to be involved from project initiation to project end.[3]

Just consider for a moment the complex skill set that the sponsor's duties demand of one individual. It is no wonder that you probably will not get the "perfect" sponsor for your project, because individuals who can deliver everything that is expected of a sponsor are few and very far between. Furthermore, even people who have the right personal qualities may not be educated in or have experience with the best practices and the intricacies of project work.

Sponsors don't just support projects; good project sponsors also support the project manager and project team. It is said that a project is one small step for a project sponsor and a giant leap for the project manager. Wouldn't we all feel so much better if we knew that the project sponsor's one small step would ensure that the complementary giant leap would lead to a safe and secure final landing?

In our experience, the skill profile of project managers continues to grow, which is a good thing, and more and more organizations are developing project managers in a disciplined and mature manner. We hope this means that accidental project managers—those who came to the role by chance and often totally unprepared—are becoming extinct. But it is also our experience that the same cannot be said of project sponsors. Far too many organizations wrongly believe that a project sponsor is just a figurehead who is never called to active duty, and so very few ever invest in any developmental support for their sponsors. Being a "good" project sponsor, like being a "good" project manager, requires structured experience, education, and guidance; but most of the time, sponsors are left with only what they have learned through happenstance throughout their careers.

This is clearly the wrong approach, and we are certain that it threatens the success of projects. According to a KPMG New Zealand project management survey released in 2010,[4] one of the main reasons for project failure is weak sponsorship:

> The project sponsor has a critical role to monitor and control the project at [the] strategic level, steering a project back on track if it runs into difficulties along the way.

> One of the fundamental reasons why projects fail is the lack of executive sponsorship and management buy-in. 68 percent of companies do not always have an effective Sponsor to provide clear direction for the project or to escalate problems when necessary.[5]

If "trying to manage a project without project management is like trying to play a football game without a game plan,"[6] then "trying to deliver a project without project sponsorship is like playing football without a rule book, a coach, any funds for new players, or even a referee."[7]

To be a successful partner on a project, a sponsor needs to be connected to the project manager and to the project team. It is a real red flag if she is remote. If she is too busy to meet, to discuss the project, and to help, the red flag turns an even darker shade. If she avoids helping assign project roles and responsibilities, or never has time to approve documents, make decisions, or just be there to advise, there is a problem—one that is reaching critical status. Throw in a dash of blaming anyone but herself for any problems, and it is probably time for you to walk away from the project if you possibly can. The project manager, the project team, and the business are in real trouble—and so is the project.

Bad sponsors will exhibit some or perhaps, in the worst-case scenario, all of the preceding behaviors. Conversely, a good project sponsor does just the opposite. She will happily act as advisor to the project manager and will focus on removing obstacles in the path to project success.

A bad project sponsor may simply be an untrained or inexperienced sponsor, but even if her poor performance is less her fault than the organization's for failing to invest in its sponsors, she still may be a project manager's worst nightmare.

WHAT DO THE PROFESSIONALS SAY?

The term *project sponsor* was first used in the early 1990s by Wendy Briner, Michael Geddes, and Colin Hastings in their book *Project Leadership*. According to the authors, a project sponsor is the project manager's boss.

They saw the sponsor as the "owner of the project, the person who pays for the work and controls the flow of money."[8] Others (Paul Dinsmore,[9] H. Curry,[10] and Ralph Kliem and Irwin Ludin[11]) saw the sponsor primarily as providing resources.

We can tell from the relatively recent appearance of the term *project sponsor* in the literature that formalization of the role is relatively new. We also know that the sponsor is the project manager's boss for this project, the owner of the project (in other words, the buck stops with her), and the person who controls the money and provides resources. Using this definition, the Spanish monarchy sponsored Christopher Columbus' journey to find an ocean route to the East Indies. Although the concept has been around for a long time, formal use of the term *project sponsor* really started only in the 1990s.

We provided PMI's definition of project sponsorship in the previous section. Now let's take a look at what two other organizations say about sponsorship. The Association for Project Management (APM) is a registered charity in the United Kingdom that develops and promotes the professional disciplines of project management and program management. APM provides a wide range of professional qualifications for the project manager. According to APM, a sponsor is

> . . . the individual or body for whom the project is undertaken and who is the primary risk taker. The sponsor owns the business case and is ultimately responsible for the project and for delivering the benefits. . . .

Project sponsorship is an active senior management role, responsible for identifying the business need, problem, or opportunity. The sponsor ensures the project remains a viable proposition and that benefits are realized, resolving any issues outside the control of the project manager.

PRINCE2 is a qualification that gives a person either *Foundation* or *Practitioner* status. In conversation with one of the authors, one of Britain's leading PRINCE2 trainers, Harminder Ahluwalia, said: "In PRINCE2, the role of the sponsor is not defined but is alluded to. The sponsor in PRINCE2 is seen as the driving force behind the project or program. The sponsor is the executive on a project board or the person appointed by the business to take ultimate responsibility for delivery of that project."

So we have three professional bodies with differing views[12]:

- PMI's definition details the expectations for the sponsor role.
- APM gives us a statement of intent.
- PRINCE2 only briefly mentions the role of the project sponsor.

WHO DOES WHAT AND WHEN?

Table I-1 outlines the project manager's and sponsor's typical roles throughout the project. This will function as a guide to begin a more detailed definition of *sponsor*. You will need to adapt the listed duties to mesh with your own companywide project management approach for specific projects. We will present a checklist that details the project sponsor's responsibilities in Chapter 2.

	Initiating	Planning	Executing	Monitoring and Control	Project Closure
Project Manager	Aids in development of the project charter Begins stakeholder identification and analysis	Develops project plans Shares with team and stakeholders Secures agreement with all on how the project will be run	Develops the project team Performs quality assurance Communicates with key stakeholders	Tracks and reports project progress Determines needed corrective actions	Closes project Conducts lessons learned assessment Organizes celebration Closes contracts Updates knowledge center with project information
Sponsor	Owner of the project case and charter Authorizes the project and project manager to begin Helps to identify high-level stakeholders, risks, project expectations, and assumptions Advises the project manager of political issues, protocols, and more	Provides input on plans Approves plans, negotiates funding Champions the project	Communicates changes in risks, issues, political climate, or anything else that may impact the project Supports the project manager and team	Actively engages in project reviews Supports corrective actions Chairs steering committee (project board) Evaluates and approves (as appropriate) change requests Checks that project is still a viable proposition Unlocks any organizational/company blockages	Participates in the celebration Provides time and resources needed for project closure Reviews postproject report to identify items relevant for future projects

TABLE I-1: The Duties of Project Managers and Sponsors

NOTES

1. The Project Management Institute's *A Guide to the Project Management Body of Knowledge (PMBOK® Guide)* presents a set of standard terminology and guidelines for project management. The *PMBOK® Guide* is process based, meaning that it describes work as being accomplished by processes. This approach is consistent with other management standards such as ISO 9000 and the Software Engineering Institute's CMMI. Processes overlap and interact throughout a project or its various phases.
2. *A Guide to the Project Management Body of Knowledge (PMBOK® Guide)*, 5th ed. (Newtown Square, PA: Project Management Institute, 2013), 32.
3. Randall L. Englund and Alfonso Bucero, *Project Sponsorship: Achieving Management Commitment for Project Success* (San Francisco: Jossey-Bass, 2006), xii.
4. The full report can be accessed at http://www.kpmg.com/NZ/en/IssuesAndInsights/ArticlesPublications/Documents/Project-Management-Survey-report.pdf.
5. The Standish Group, *Chaos Manifesto 2012: The Year of the Executive Sponsor* (Boston: The Standish Group, 2012), 3.
6. Karen Tate, PMP, a past board member of PMI. Collected on the Project Auditors LLC website: http://www.projectauditors.com/Company/Project_Management_Quotes.html.
7. Penned by Peter Taylor for publication in this volume.
8. Lynn Crawford and Christine Brett, "Exploring the Role of the Project Sponsor" (Sydney, Australia: University of Technology, 2000), Project Management Program website: http://www.projects.uts.edu.au/resources/pdfs/PMINZ2001CrawfordBrett.pdf.
9. Paul C. Dinsmore, *The AMA Handbook of Project Management* (New York: AMACOM, 1993).
10. H. Curry, "Project Sponsorship," *PM Network* (Newtown Square, PA: Project Management Institute, March 1995).
11. Ralph L. Kliem, Irwin S. Ludin, and Ken L. Robertson, *Project Management Methodology, a Practical Guide for the Millenium* (New York: Marcel Dekker, 1997).
12. All three bodies are continuing to develop their views on sponsorship.

A project is one small step for the project sponsor, one giant leap for the project manager.

PART I
For the Project Manager

CHAPTER 1
Preparing to Work with Your Sponsor

How many project managers get to choose the projects they manage? Not many. The project allocation process in most companies just doesn't work that way, does it?

Now, how many project managers get to choose the project sponsors they work with? Probably none. Again, it just doesn't work that way in most, perhaps any, organizations. You won't get the opportunity to ask a sponsor for her résumé and put her through a formal interview process—nice as it would be to say, "I'm sorry, but I just don't think that this is the job for you right now," if she isn't a great fit for the position.

But perhaps you can, through your experience and your relationships with executive management, request a particular person you know you can work effectively with to partner with you once again on your next project. You also can try to educate the decision-makers about how to select the best possible project sponsor. You may be able to influence the way the organization selects and assigns sponsors by sharing some high-level definitions and expectations of the sponsor role based on this book and other best practices. (Chapter 6 provides more information on these concepts.)

Even if you don't have the perfect sponsor, you can prepare to work with the one you have by knowing what you're in for and making sure you get off to a good start.

WHO SHOULD SPONSOR YOUR PROJECT?

Make a judgment call on what competencies this particular project requires. Is the project simple or complex? Should you ask to be assigned the sponsor you want, or can you risk working with a new (perhaps good, perhaps not) sponsor on this project? There are probably several people within the organization who could be good sponsors for your project. The following criteria will help you work with executive management to appoint the person most likely to guide the project to success:

- Who has the greatest interest in the outcomes of the project?

- Who has the greatest influence with the high-level stakeholders of the project?

- Does this person have proven experience in sponsoring projects?

- Does this person have the capacity to be an effective collaborator and leader for the project manager and project team?

- Does this person have education and experience in project management best practices?

- Does this person trust those around him to act in the best interest of the project?

If the same person is named in your responses to questions 1 and 2, and you can answer yes to the remaining questions, you have your sponsor.

If the person named in your answers to 1 and 2 is not capable of sponsoring the project, look for a trusted delegate to assign as sponsor, or negotiate and document the roles of the delegate (the more capable person) and the sponsor (the more influential person).

If you name different people when answering questions 1 and 2, select the more appropriate sponsor based on the answers to the remaining questions.

Remember that lacking competencies can be mitigated through sponsor education. Help the sponsor understand what is in it for her and how these competencies can maximize the chance for project success.

ASSESSING YOUR SPONSOR

Let's say you've been assigned a project and a sponsor, and that is that. You're left to deal with what you've been given. It is said that you cannot manage what you don't measure, and that is as true for project sponsors as it is for anything. So let's start there: how can you assess your project sponsor? In this book, we give you a variety of checklists to help you to understand your project sponsor (see later chapters and appendixes). Below, we detail other tools you as the project manager can use to better understand your sponsor and then to adapt your communication style and project approach to make the most of her skills.

THE POWER GRID

You can use the power grid shown in Figure 1-1 to assess your newly assigned sponsor—specifically her interest in your project (from high to low) and her actual power in your organization (also from high to low). This may well be challenging to determine early on—especially if you have never worked with this sponsor beforehand—however you can update your assessment as you personally get to know your sponsor better and you build a relationship.

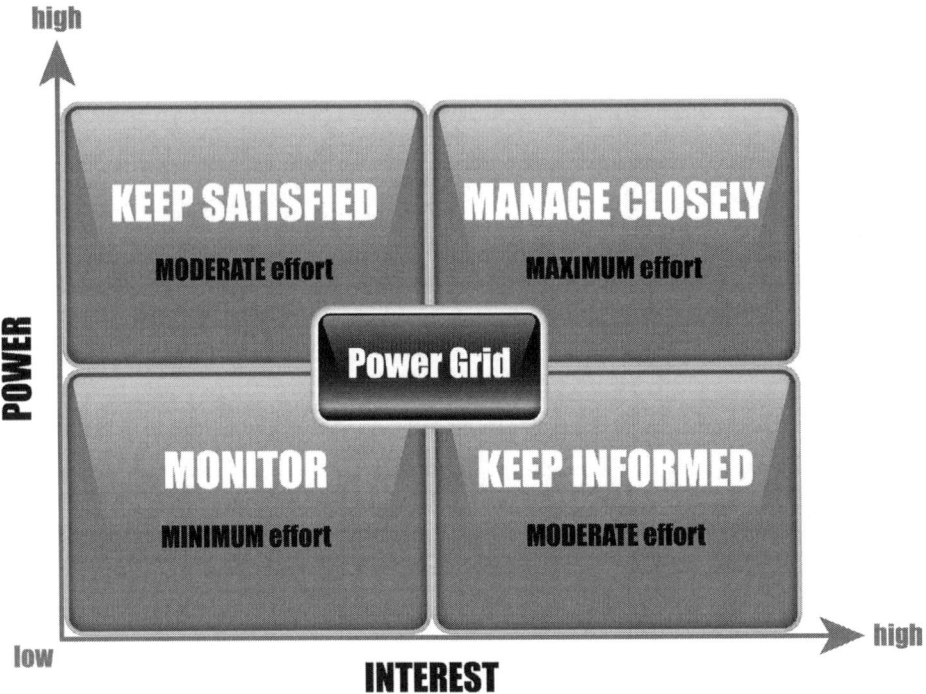

FIGURE 1-1: Power Grid for Assessing Sponsors

Initially, though, you can use your past observations of this sponsor (if you have any), current discussions (that you are undertaking with the sponsor—you are on that learning curve already), and peer responses (you can ask your colleague project managers about the sponsor if they have worked with her on past projects).

The power grid suggests general courses of action you can try to manage your relationship with any sponsor.

If your project sponsor falls into the "low interest, low power" quadrant, you really have a problem. It is unlikely that this sponsor will ever support your project management endeavors; even if she could be persuaded to, her influence is so weak that her cooperation is not worth pursuing.

On the other hand, a "high interest, high power" sponsor can be very useful indeed. However, she will also have to be managed carefully, because her high interest in the project could lead to micromanagement and long, overly detailed update meetings. This is not something that a project manager wishes to encourage.

Let's take a closer look at specific strategies for managing to the power grid:

- **Manage closely.** This sponsor is very interested in what is going on with your project and has great influence over it. As such, she should always have the most current information on project progress and challenges and should be able to provide the helicopter view—i.e., whether it sits with the overall strategy of what is going on. Reporting to this sponsor may mean daily emails and weekly meetings. The danger of not "managing closely" is that trust will not be optimized, thereby creating a risk for micromanagement from the sponsor.

- **Keep satisfied.** Find out what your project sponsor expects and meet those needs. The goal is to provide enough information that she feels informed but not so much that she feels burdened. Make requests of her only when there are no other channels, and come armed with a completed analysis of options already considered.

- **Keep informed.** Interested sponsors require information, so make sure you have processes in place so they know about progress and challenges and how to easily gain further information of they feel that they need it. This includes weekly status updates and regularly scheduled meetings.

- **Monitor.** Ask questions of your sponsor to ensure she feels informed, knowledgeable, and included in the project. This sponsor may not be keeping up with the project progress and status, so your challenge is to make sure that she both understands and appropriately acts on project successes and challenges when needed.

TYPES OF POWER

All project stakeholders—indeed, anyone in an organization—can hold one or more types of power. Which of the following does your sponsor have? Which do you have?

- **Legitimate:** power endowed by a formal title or position (authority)
- **Reward:** power held by those who are able to impose positive consequences (carrot)
- **Coercive:** power held by those who can impose negative consequences (stick)
- **Financial:** power held by those who control the budget (money)
- **Bureaucratic:** power held by those with knowledge of the system (intelligence)
- **Referent:** power endowed by association with someone else's power (network)
- **Technical:** power held by those who have technical knowledge relating to the project (skill)
- **Charismatic:** power granted through personality alone (character).

You and your sponsor can work together to use her (and your) power how and when you need to. But use it sparingly and use it wisely.

Let's take a closer look at these types of power and how they can be used:

- **Legitimate power.** Regardless of the type of organization—hierarchical or matrix—in which you work, the more senior a person is, the greater the opportunity to assert authority and cause things to happen. This power should be used sparingly.

- **Reward power.** Commonly used to engage resources and stakeholders, this power may be used at the start of a project as part of a marketing activity or later in the project to focus efforts and meet a deliverable milestone. Rewards can be offered directly from the sponsor or through you, the project manager, as fits the situation. Rewards can also be offered for good work or given as surprise "thank-yous" to good contributors.

- **Coercive power.** Perhaps the least used type, this will likely achieve what you and your sponsor want but not gain ongoing cooperation. Often it can be better to offer the "carrot" alongside the "stick."

- **Financial power.** In many cases this type of power allows application of the "reward" power but can lead to a declaration that "this is my budget (and my project) and I will apply it as I see fit"—a kind of "take it or leave it" negotiation position.

- **Bureaucratic power.** By understanding how things work inside your organization and aligning requirements with mandated processes (such as matters of compliance and regulatory authority), you can use this type of power to make and enforce decisions.

- **Referent power.** This is the "my dad is bigger than your dad" style of argument. The stronger a person's network, the greater the inferred authority. This authority comes not from the power and influence of an individual but from that of associates.

- **Technical power.** A key role of any successful project manager is to understand the critical details. Those who possess this knowledge have the advantage.

- **Charismatic power.** Both the project sponsor and the project manager can gain a lot of favors through being positive, engaging, and likeable. If you are fun to work with, viewed as successful, and considered influential, this power will get people on your side.

You may be wondering how you and your sponsor can work together to leverage the types of power you both possess. You will find the answers in just about any cop show, but "good cop, bad cop" is just one example: the bad cop uses coercive power to try to scare the criminal into submission while the good cop uses reward and charisma to show what good can come of a full confession.

You will find that you may have any or many of these types of power at your disposal given the situation. Project sponsors and project managers often fall into particular types of power according to their position in the organization:

- **Project sponsor**
    - Legitimate
    - Coercive
    - Financial

- o Bureaucratic
- o Charismatic

- **Project manager**
  - o Legitimate
  - o Reward
  - o Technical
  - o Referent
  - o Charismatic

A project sponsor may use legitimate and coercive power to get team members to the table, but the project manager will get a better result by combining those powers with technical and charismatic power to earn their trust and desired participation. On the other hand, you may have great technical power but need to call upon your project sponsor with bureaucratic power to help mitigate a risk to the project from another division. Work to enhance the powers that come naturally to you and the situation while learning to leverage the power of your project sponsor to complement it. Together, you can be the perfect partnership or the dynamic duo.

INTERVIEWING THE SPONSOR

More often than not, the project sponsor has been chosen by the business well before you have even been selected as the project manager. However, if the company has a strong project management culture, this idea is entirely plausible. If, of course, your company does *not* have a strong project management culture, the interviewing of a possible sponsor for your project is something for you to work on!

But let's just assume for one magical moment that you could interview her; this could be fun. **Suspend your disbelief and go with it.** What if a prospective sponsor answered your questions as follows?

Q: Tell me why you think you are the right person for this job.

A: Well, what skills are you looking for in a good project sponsor?

Q: What strengths will you bring to the role?

A: What are the strengths that would make your life as a project manager that much easier?

Q: What are your weak points, and what actions will you take to address these issues?

A: What weaknesses are you looking to avoid at all costs?

To this, you might reply, "You know, I'm sorry, but based on your experience, I think it is better if I look elsewhere for my project sponsor this time around. Thank you for your interest." (Of course, you can only dream of saying this!)

You may actually be able to get answers to a few of these questions by indicating that you want to leverage your strengths and weaknesses against hers. You also should be prepared to answer these questions yourself so that you can look at your own strengths and weaknesses.

This chapter is titled "preparing to work with your sponsor." If you are indeed to prepare, then you need data. You can assess the sponsor using the tools mentioned and others presented further on in the book. However, wouldn't it be useful to you, the project manager, to understand where the sponsor has strengths and development needs?

In the box below, we present a variety of candidates put forward for a sponsor role. You may never get the opportunity to formally interview your sponsor. However, you may need to understand your sponsor just that little bit more, and we believe the ideas below will help. Don't forget: an interview can reveal development needs—something you can help the sponsor with!

> **INTERVIEWING SPONSOR CANDIDATES**
>
> Imagine that you have the opportunity to interview four potential project sponsors for your project. Once you have heard from all four, you can elect to take further action to help you decide, or you can make an immediate decision.
>
> ### Candidate 1
>
> I have been working at this company for five years and have progressed to the executive level in the last year. I haven't as yet sponsored a project, but I am keen to get the first one under my belt. Your project seems pretty interesting and quite important to the company, and it would be great to work with you on this.
>
> I have a reasonable amount of time to spend on it, apart from a three-week vacation the month after next, but aside from that, I am there for you as you need me.
>
> I'm not too fond of long meetings, so I would suggest we catch up by phone every week or so—or perhaps you would suggest something different; you are the expert, after all.
>
> ### Candidate 2
>
> You know me pretty well, since we worked together on Project Phoenix a year or so ago. I know it was a bit of a rough ride, but we mostly got there in the end. I do have experience in project sponsorship, I understand this whole project-based activity thing, and I am right behind this particular initiative. In fact, I was the main voice on the approval board to get it up and running.

Since we last worked together, I sponsored the new expense management project, and that went live only last month.

It seems like it makes a lot of sense for us to join forces once again and get this one delivered for the business.

Candidate 3

I'm glad I could make this meeting—I just love working with you project managers, and this would be my fourth project sponsor role right now. This is a key role, as you know, and I want to bring my experience and authority to bear in order for you to do your bit successfully. Sponsoring a project is all about getting people pointing in the right direction and providing the occasional kick to anyone who gets in your way. You just let me know who, and I'll sort it out for you.

Candidate 4

[Candidate 4 apologizes for being unable to make the interview, as he is responding to an urgent work situation. He did say that he has past experience as a sponsor and would be eager to support this project when it starts.]

Action

You now have to decide what to do next. Can you decide which sponsor you want to work with now, or is there more that you need to know?

- Write down your plan of action.
- Will you reject any sponsor candidate now?
- What steps will you take to reach a point of decision?
- Whom do you favor at this point in time?

Suggested Plans

Here is one possible way of looking at the candidates.

Let's start with candidate 4. Even though he could not make the interview, he does have experience and appears to be focused on urgent matters. You may well decide that he is worth a little more effort and reach out to his peers for more information. What specific experience does he have, how did his projects progress, and what do the project managers he's worked with have to say about him? As for the "urgent work situation"—was it really urgent, or was it just an excuse? If you like what your research reveals, then you may have a good candidate to consider; if not, then perhaps it's best to reject him.

Candidate 1 seems enthusiastic, but on the downside, she has no experience as a sponsor and, while she is at the executive level now, she's pretty new and perhaps might not have the necessary influence yet. She has preferences regarding communication but also seems open to your guidance.

Candidate 2 has a track record, and you have personal experience working with her. It was not a particularly positive experience, but maybe "better the devil you know" applies. At the very least, you should talk to the project manager for the expense system project and see if she exhibited the same behavior that made working with her difficult, or perhaps she has learned how to be a better project sponsor in the interim. On the positive side, she seems to believe in this new project, as she was a strong supporter in the approval phase.

Candidate 3 appears to collect projects as a hobby, but does he really understand the role of sponsor, and can he really sponsor so many projects at one time? What if there are conflicts between the projects—how will he manage this? You might look into the timing of his other projects and see if some are coming to an end any time soon. You would need this sponsor to agree not to take any more projects on while yours is running.

> You may want to assess the past performance of all of the candidates you put on your short list using the checklist of sponsor responsibilities introduced in Chapter 2, based on personal observation, postproject reviews, and information from peers. And remember, you will also gain valuable insight by asking them about their hopes for and fears about the project.

KICKING OFF YOUR RELATIONSHIP WITH THE SPONSOR

It has often been said that it is people who deliver projects. We appreciate the need for really strong processes to ensure effective delivery. However, we also know that for projects to be delivered, we must work with and through other people. This means helping to develop rapport with others, including the project sponsor, the project team, senior-level people in the organization, and all manner of project stakeholders. By *rapport*, we mean the feeling that "occurs when two or more people feel that they are in sync or on the same wavelength because they feel similar or relate well to each other."[1]

MAKING THE MOST OF THE FIRST MEETING

One of the authors was in training with Stuart. Stuart worked for the company and was to become the company project management expert and one-man PMO. He said that project managers needed a key skill—the ability to "raise their head above the parapet." He meant that sometimes project managers need to go outside their comfort zones. They need to ask awkward questions and deal with completely arbitrary delivery dates (set in offices that are often a long way from the project), among many other difficult duties. They need to use their professional judgment to resolve a host of potential problems. One of these problems can be headed off ahead of time: lack of knowledge and understanding of the sponsor's needs, style, ambitions, and objectives.

Knowledge is power. Why enter into a working relationship with your new project sponsor in a state of ignorance? Planning and preparation before your first meeting with the sponsor goes a long way to making the meeting a success. By success, we mean not just that you get along and enjoy a civilized chat about the project, but rather that you leave the meeting with the information you need to work effectively with the sponsor in the coming months.

But how can you prepare for such a meeting? Assuming that the sponsor is new to you, there are a number of things that you can do before your first meeting. Doing nothing beforehand makes no sense at all.

Start by considering her project sponsorship experience. Now, this does not mean that you should conduct an investigation into your new sponsor—don't hire a private eye just yet! It just means that you can subtly and quietly gather some intelligence from

- Project manager peers (who may have worked with her as a sponsor beforehand)
- Other project sponsors (with whom you have worked and who may know this person)
- Executive managers (with whom you have a good working relationship).

Ask about the successes and the challenges that the sponsor has faced, how she responded to any problems, and how she supported project manager(s) she has worked with.

Be sure to also look into any project-based experience she may have. Maybe you will strike gold and connect with a project sponsor who has a project management background. This does not necessarily mean that she will be a good project sponsor, but it will mean that she appreciates the "thrill" of the project world and the special challenges that can be thrown the way of a project manager.

Finally, try to get a view of her management style and the authority that she carries within the organization. This will help you assess her as a sponsor and determine the particular ways in which she can be helpful to you.

Now that you know something about your sponsor, what should you expect and how should you behave in that critical first face-to-face meeting? What is important to cover now, and what can wait until later on?

In this first meeting, you have two major objectives:

- Develop a relationship and rapport with your project sponsor that sets the stage for successful collaboration throughout the project.
- Begin capturing important information that will be used to formally begin the project (i.e., to develop the project charter or other initiation document).

When preparing for the first meeting with your sponsor, you need to understand that some sponsors will have a very fixed vision for the project and will tell you, and the rest of the project team, exactly what they want, when they want it, and what will happen if they don't get what they want. Be cautious with these sponsors; their strength of purpose and character may challenge your interviewing skills. Even if your sponsor makes things difficult, persevere until you have agreed on a purpose, which you need to run the project, and work closely with him. Use your newness to the project and ignorance to your advantage. Ask the sponsor to help you understand the drivers for the project and what benefit she expects to achieve.

Other project sponsors may have a vision that appears to be an undefined conceptual possibility, developed, perhaps, with a small dose of delusion. Again, you have to apply control and discipline to reach the level of understanding and detail that you need in order to be an effective manager of the project.

The initial meeting is where you will set the tone for the relationship with your project sponsor for the rest of the project. This is your opportunity to impress her with your professionalism and expertise. We will walk you through an agenda for this initial meeting that will make you look good and give your project sponsor confidence in your abilities.

THE AGENDA

Likely attendees include the project manager, project sponsor, business owner/customer, lead business analyst, and others as appropriate. Topics you may want to cover include the following:

- Business objective
- Anticipated impact of project deliverables
- Quality expectations
- Risks
- Business drivers
- Stakeholders
- Constraints (budget, dates, policy, other)

- Time commitment

- Decision-making

- Supporting the team

- Communications planning

- Mutual understanding of the assumptions that have been made in developing the business case and expected outcomes.

Peter discusses the first seven bullets in his book *The Lazy Project Manager*[2]; here, we will focus on relationship building.

Admittedly, this suggested agenda is quite full—you may need to have a number of meetings to cover all of the topics, or you can explore other ways to elicit information from, or share information with, your sponsor.

ASKING THE QUESTIONS YOU NEED TO ASK

Going back to the second primary objective of your first meeting with the sponsor—beginning to capture important information that will be used to formally begin the project—consider the topics listed above.

Remember, first impressions really count, so be sure to prepare well. If you conduct yourself in a professional, confident manner in your first meeting with your sponsor, you will not only make a positive impression by demonstrating your capability, but you will also provide a valuable service to the sponsor by bringing your expertise and project experience to the forefront of the project.

One tip here: you are only in the information-gathering phase right now, and while you do want to manage the project with a firm hand from day one, you have to be sensitive at this first meeting. We advise being a little gentle to begin with, at least until you understand what type of sponsor you are dealing with. Now is the time to just observe the sponsor and determine what style of communication and kind of relationship she expects from you. You can put a firm grip in place and negotiate hard later on. Right now, just learn and inwardly digest what you are told.

DETERMINING WHAT'S IN IT FOR THE SPONSOR

You need to understand, if you don't already, what is in it for your sponsor—what her previous experience as a sponsor has been like, both in terms of her knowledge about being a sponsor and her real project experience (i.e., was a previous project a nightmare project?). Even if she has never sponsored before, she will, no doubt, have an opinion of sponsoring based upon stories she's heard about past projects and from other executives. Determine her willingness to learn more about project sponsorship and the best way to help coach her (e.g., reading this book, receiving just-in-time feedback, or attending training).

Manage your sponsor well, and he will be your ally in the coming weeks and months.

OPEN DISCUSSION WORKS

Feel free to start the conversation at the first meeting in a simple way, with an open question—for example, "Tell me about the project." Active listening is an underutilized skill in communication. Use it now. There is enormous value in asking your sponsor to answer just two (apparently) simple questions:

- What are your hopes for the project?
- What are your fears about the project?

You will gain a lot of insight into how the sponsor feels about the project and the challenges you may have to plan for in the coming weeks and months by asking these questions. The answers will also help you capture data for project initiation without getting "technical" right away.

Open questions have the following characteristics:

- They ask the respondent to think and reflect.
- They are designed to elicit the respondent's opinions and feelings.
- They hand control of the conversation to the respondent.
- They are likely to receive long answers (this is true of any question, but open questions deliberately seek longer answers).

ASKING ABOUT THE SPONSOR'S EXPECTATIONS

You have already talked with others about your sponsor's experience and approach, while avoiding taking at face value any secondhand statements or rumors about her views and expectations. To find out what she really wants and expects, you have to speak with her directly and take only her word regarding her expectations. It may well be possible that the sponsor does not yet know what she expects. Perhaps this is her first time as a project sponsor and the role is as new to her as she is to you. If that is the case, you need to help her and guide her in his responsibilities.

Once you have a broad understanding of the sponsor's feelings about this particular project and an idea of what she expects from you and the project, you can follow up with other questions to reach a suitable level of confidence in your understanding of the key topics.

TIME COMMITMENT

Obviously, the project sponsor must devote time to the project if it is to have the greatest chance of success. Have an open conversation about the time commitment so you can reach agreement about it before the sponsor's project responsibilities begin. The amount of time the sponsor will need to spend will vary project by project, depending on size, risk, and complexity. This could be anywhere from one hour a day for a high-risk, highly complex project to 30 minutes once per month for simple projects. Your project sponsor should be ready to commit to a minimum of 30 minutes per month to discuss project status.

This is a good time to make sure the sponsor understands that there may be periods when she will need to spend more time than usual on the project. Let her know that you are conscious her time and that you will not be asking for her attention frivolously.

Now also is the time to find out who the trusted delegates of the project sponsor are and their level of authority. Schedule the 30-minutes-a-month minimum even if the sponsor fully delegates all aspects of the project. The only way to be sure that the project sponsor is fully aware of status and issues is to meet with her personally. Include sponsor delegates in the meeting to keep communications open and maintain trust.

DECISION-MAKING

Any project will frequently require that your project sponsor make decisions. A delay in a decision can have a significant impact on the project schedule. Talk about this with your project sponsor and help her understand how crucial timely decisions are in keeping a project on track. Work to get agreement that the sponsor will make needed decisions within 24 hours.

Failing to make a decision in that time frame may result in a project change request to adjust the schedule for the delay.

Find out what your sponsor will generally want from you and the project team to keep her commitment on decision-making. Will she want full details and copies of all of the relevant documents? Perhaps she will simply want a summary of the issue with a recommended action, or a list of options that the team has already explored from which she will choose. If you know her general preference, you can proactively prepare and give her what she needs. Keep in mind that she may ask for different information or recommendations for any given risk.

Having this discussion early to set guidelines and establish a common understanding of the sponsor's information needs will go a long way toward helping her provide decision support throughout the project. We have noticed that communication within projects and project management in particular tends to be poor. It takes time, planning, and a commitment by the project manager and team. Only then will trends in reporting of communications improve (and improve they must!).

TEAM SUPPORT

Your project sponsor may not be aware of how valuable her public and private support of the team can be for the project. Staffers who understand how they are contributing to the greater good of the organization will perform better and have better morale. Nothing sets the tone for this more than a project sponsor who takes an active interest in the team. Taking an active interest does not mean that team members should begin going to the project sponsor instead of the project manager with concerns, but only that each contribution is valued by the sponsor and therefore the organization.

Let your sponsor know that simple acts can go a long way in supporting the team. She can

- Speak at the project kickoff about the project, its purpose, what changes she anticipates, and her appreciation of those contributing to it.
- Meet team members, ask what they do on the project, and remember them.
- Acknowledge team members when she sees them at the water cooler.
- Ask how the project is going and if they have any concerns. (Concerns need to be resolved through the project manager, but that does not mean the sponsor cannot care about them.)
- Send a personal note or email of appreciation when she hears of good work or extra effort from team members.
- Support efforts to identify project stakeholders and their management. (This is particularly important for the "political" stakeholders the project manager may not be aware of.)
- Attend a milestone or retrospective meeting to thank the team in person (bringing goodies doesn't hurt).
- Always acknowledge the team and its efforts when speaking to others about the project.

COMMUNICATIONS PLANNING

Being the best project manager for your sponsor will take a lot of planning, particularly communications planning. Some 80 to 90 percent of what we do as project managers is communicate. Planning ahead about *how* you will communicate will take much of the work out of the actual communications throughout the project.

Let's take a look at the results of a ten-year survey conducted by the project management training and consultancy company Project Agency.[3] Almost 1,500 people were asked whether they agreed that the following statement regarding communication in their projects was true: "Communication is such that people are always aware of changing priorities." The results are shown in Figure 1-2; more data are available in Appendix A.

The survey participants clearly suggested that communication within their projects is poor. Corroborating this, we have heard some very negative comments about communication from people who have attended our project management courses. Typically, they say that communication in projects reflects communication in the business—it's all generally poor.

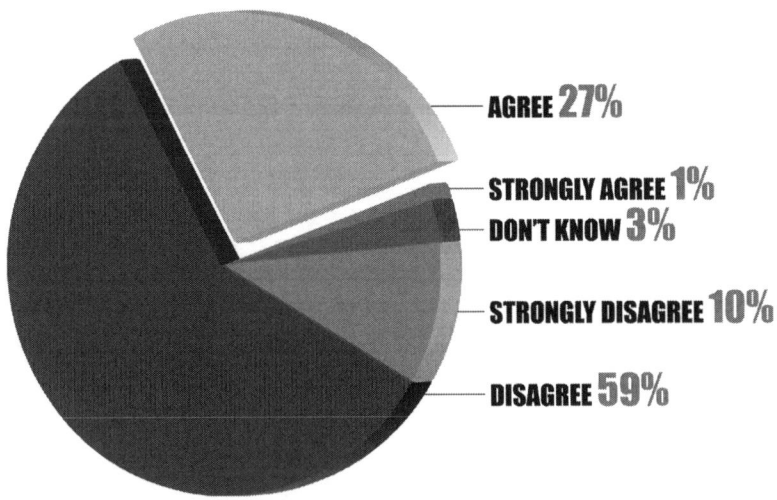

FIGURE 1-2: Effectiveness of Communication

But a project manager who is striving to be the best does not just accept weak communication within projects. It's essential to think about, trial, and put into play key plans for communication. As you develop plans for communicating with your sponsor, think about what you're trying to achieve:

- Get a decision on something

- Seek advice from someone who has a different perspective

- Talk about a problem and make a recommendation or suggestion

- Go through the agreed-upon reporting process

- Suggest that she open a door for you: "I really need to see someone in Human Resources—whom do you suggest, and how?"

You will have to develop a clearly defined plan for communicating in any situation that's likely to arise.

One of the many benefits of planning communication is preventing the parties from falling into the trap of resorting to type. For example, let's say you prefer to talk face-to-face with people and do so as much as possible. Under pressure, you may feel as if a face-to-face conversation is the best or only way to deal with a concern, but face-to-face communication is not always feasible or the best approach in every case. Developing a specific communication plan that states how you'll communicate about particular project elements will help you avoid resorting to your preferred method if it's not the most effective one for the situation.

How can you get started devising a communication plan? We have often used an exercise with teams that will work equally well with your project sponsor. It is a simple round-robin discussion where each person answers the following questions:

- What is your preferred method of communication?
- What is the best way to alert you of something urgent?
- How will I know when you are stressed?
- What is the best thing I can do when you are stressed?
- What else should I know about you?

The answers are recorded, shared, and kept in a common place where they can easily be referenced. If others who are familiar with your sponsor are in the room when you're asking her these questions, ask them for their input regarding her communication style. This often brings out feedback that may surprise the sponsor.

After you've gathered the above information, work to get agreement on communication guidelines before the project gets underway. Getting basic information on preferences should be part of your initial discussions with your project sponsor and key stakeholders. Start a communications matrix, like the sample plan in Figure 1-3, that describes the project elements about which you will need to communicate, how you'll communicate about each one, and how frequent those communications will be. Then walk through the plan with your sponsor to elicit his feedback and make adjustments as needed.

Keep the following in mind regarding communicating with your sponsor:

- You are responsible for submitting a communications plan.
- Think of new, efficient ways that you can share information with your sponsor. Perhaps you can text or instant-message urgent information, share status updates on an organization bulletin board, or create a group page on a common social media site such as LinkedIn or Facebook.

	Project Element	How to Communicate	How Frequently to Communicate?
1	Monitoring the project	a. Submit highlight report. b. Meet with sponsor.	a. Highlight reports every 2 weeks. b. Meet with sponsor every 4 weeks unless problems arise, which will initially be communicated via an email asking for a meeting.
2	Risk management	Submit updated risk logs to sponsor for comments and concerns.	Every week to sponsor; every week from sponsor about concerns, etc.
3	Decision-making	Done on basis of highlight reports and risk log. Project manager to make decisions where he can but will take those outside authority to sponsor. Project manager cannot make changes that challenge scope, budget, or business benefits.	As required, but based on biweekly highlight report or project-monitoring meeting schedule.
4	Networking with different stakeholders	Sponsor to do this on basis of plan submitted by project manager.	Frequency based on communications plan put together by project manager.

FIGURE 1-3: Sample Communications Plan

- Once you know what methods your sponsor prefers, use those approaches, but supplement them with other methods as needed.

- Use multiple channels—for example, email as well as in-person meetings—for communicating with your sponsor.

- If you think you are over-communicating, ask your sponsor. She may begin to disregard your messages if she thinks you are overdoing it.

- If your sponsor simply does not want to engage in any way, this is a risk to the project. Put the problem in your risk log and let your sponsor know! This is tough but very necessary for your project and your sanity. It may open the door to talking with the sponsor about ways he can meet the project's needs, such as through delegation.

- You will need to invest more time in communicating with inexperienced sponsors.

- If you are working with a bureaucratic sponsor, she will expect (indeed demand) that you complete the right project management paperwork at the right time and in the prescribed manner. Any delay in supplying this will possibly delay the project. Your communications to the sponsor are through the project documentation and need to be right. Work to her strengths!

- If you're working with a detail-oriented sponsor, be sure to supply the type of information she requires. Keep backup information in your hip pocket, so to speak, when meeting with her.

- Remember, your goal is to be the best project manager for your sponsor. Consider leadership guru John Kotter's advice: "Good communication does not mean that you have to speak in perfectly formed sentences and paragraphs. It isn't about slickness. Simple and clear go a long way."[4]

NOTES

1. Wikipedia, "Rapport," http://en.wikipedia.org/wiki/Rapport.
2. Peter Taylor, *The Lazy Project Manager* (Oxford: Infinite Ideas, 2009). This book illustrates how people can apply the simple techniques of "lazy" project management to their own activities in order to work more effectively and consequently improve work–life balance. The approach of "productive laziness" builds on the Pareto principle, which states that for many phenomena, 80 percent of consequences stem from 20 percent of the causes. To put it simply, only 20 percent of the things people do during their working days really matter.

3   Project Agency is a London-based project management consultancy led by Ron Rosenhead, a coauthor of this book. (More information is available at www.projectagency.co.uk.)
4   *Harvard Business School Bulletin* [online] (February 2001), http://www.alumni.hbs.edu/bulletin/2001/february/kotter.html.

CHAPTER 2
Working with a Sponsor

You already know that sponsors are generally busy, in-demand people, and your project is just one activity among many that your sponsor is currently working on. She will want everything from you that you want from her. She doesn't want an absent project manager, an inexperienced project manager, an untrained project manager, or a micromanaging project manager—and she certainly doesn't want a project manager who wants to be the project sponsor.

What she does want is confidence that everything is under control, that you will keep her informed as required, and that you will use her time, knowledge, influence, and power wisely and with discretion. If you can manage to become her trusted advisor on all matters regarding the project, you will be her go-to person. If, however, you escalate every problem to her, no matter how small or trivial, and if you won't make a decision without her consent, then you are not doing your job as a project manager. (On the other hand, don't wait until you are on the very edge of a crisis or project failure to go to her—too little, too late.)

Most senior managers are capable of being and willing to be good sponsors, but sometimes they need a little help from you. They certainly don't want you to demand 100 percent of their time, nor can they afford to provide it. At the same time, it's essential to go out of your way to involve the sponsor. There is no doubt that in the early days of the project, this will take up more of your time than perhaps you feel you can afford, but it will lay the foundation for a great, trusting relationship with your sponsor that will pay dividends later on in the project. And imagine how smoothly the next project you collaborate on will go if you both get it right this time around.

USING YOUR INFLUENCE

You're trying to deliver a technical project, and we are asking you to think about influencing your sponsor. Running technical projects and influencing others are very far removed from each other—or are they?

If you cannot influence the selection of your sponsor, then you can consider influencing her behavior, should that be required. One of your primary goals in your relationship with your sponsor should be to make her feel as if it is in her interest to be a good sponsor for you and your project. You will need a strategy for dealing with someone who is probably very busy, is not necessarily engaged, and who has received little or no training in sponsorship (and project management).

You can immediately discount using financial means to influence your sponsor (not a good career move), so what else can you try? There is no right or wrong way to influence people; you simply have to discover the best method for each individual situation to achieve a positive result.

The types of influence you can try when working with your sponsor (or anyone else in your organization, including other executives) can be categorized in four ways: direct influence, influence through appeal, persuasion, and social influence. Within each category, there are several distinct approaches.

DIRECT INFLUENCE

The Request Approach

Make a direct statement of your need that is based on solid research and is substantiated by fact. When delivering your request, you must be confident, positive, polite, and firm.

The Legitimacy Approach

Show that what you want is consistent with organizational (or project) policy and procedures. For people to respond well to this approach, you need to refer to specific policies and procedures or management requests or directives as a basis for your decision. You might cite higher management when making your request, but consider your project sponsor's position in the hierarchy when you do this and be sensitive to any potential insult you might deliver by referencing higher-ups.

INFLUENCE THROUGH APPEAL

The Value Approach

You can inspire cooperation by making an appeal to the sponsor's values, emotions, or feelings. Demonstrate personal enthusiasm, commitment, dedication, and passion. Take a motivational or inspirational approach: Speak in terms of achievement, quality, or other desired values. Appeal to his sense of loyalty, a cause he cares about, or just being part of a winning team. (All values you focus on should apply to your project.) Strive to build trust and find common ground. Remember, people at advanced levels of their careers aspire to excel at what they do. Demonstrate how your ideas will help them excel.

The Friendship Approach

When the most expedient way to get what you need is by asking for it as a personal favor, you will use the friendship approach. This approach depends on relationships and loyalty, so it probably will not work with most sponsors. Indeed, if the two of you have a good track record of working together over a number of projects, you may have less need to influence the sponsor. For this approach to work, you must recognize and acknowledge any inconvenience your request may cause, and you must be willing to reciprocate at some point in the future.

The Consulting Approach

This approach is about appealing to the sponsor's expertise and experience and asking for his intervention. If this approach is to work, you will need to prepare your proposal and state it in broad terms to allow a lot of latitude in the sponsor's response. You must listen to the person's response and ask open-ended questions.

PERSUASION

The Exchange Approach

The exchange approach is about giving the sponsor something of value (but remember, not money!) in return for what you want or need for the project. You should negotiate an exchange of favors to create a win-win situation for you and the sponsor. For the sponsor to respond well to this approach, you must find out what his likely needs are and then plan an exchange intended to satisfy those needs.

The Logic Approach

Here, you use logic or clear evidence to justify a request and gain the support of the sponsor. For this approach to work, make sure your request is well researched and supported by facts.

SOCIAL INFLUENCE

The Social Approach

This is simply behaving in a warm and friendly manner in order to build a supportive rapport and thus influence the sponsor. (Be sure not to be overly familiar—remember your professional boundaries and respect the sponsor's position within the organization.) For this approach to be effective, you need to be consistently friendly—don't run hot and cold when interacting with the sponsor.

The Allegiance Approach

In this approach, you assemble a group to influence the sponsor. This really is an extreme approach and not one to use lightly. The sponsor probably will not like it much, so apply it only when there is no other approach left open to you. If this approach is to work, you must get one (or more) influential peers on board—people that the sponsor is known to respect.

The Modeling Approach

You can inspire the sponsor to behave in a certain way by setting an example through your own behavior. This approach can work if you treat others with respect, empathy, and consideration, and you practice what you preach.

ASKING YOUR SPONSOR FOR HELP

Life is considerably easier when you have worked out a practical plan for interacting with your sponsor. But what happens if you urgently need your sponsor's help?

Start by explaining why you need her assistance, and be clear about what exactly you need. Be prepared to answer the following questions:

- Why can't you resolve the issue yourself?
- What have you tried already?
- What were the outcomes of those efforts?
- What do you need from me now?
- When do you need it?
- Why do you need it?

It may seem obvious to you what you need and why you need it, but assume that your sponsor needs more information than that. Executives really hate being asked to make a complicated and important decision without all of the facts. They also hate being asked to make a complicated and important decision on the spot, without any advance warning and without any time to think about it. Notify your sponsor ahead of time, if you can, that you need help.

Emergencies do happen on projects, so it is critical that you have a) built a good foundation of trust with your project sponsor so that she takes you at face value when and if such an emergency occurs and b) prepared her at the start of the project and your relationship that there may come a time when you will need something or some decision fast and now.

GIVING FEEDBACK TO YOUR SPONSOR

There may be times when you have to talk to your sponsor about something she has done, or not done, that has caused the project problems. Giving and receiving feedback, no matter how well intentioned it is, can be tough. It's significantly harder still to give feedback to your "project boss," someone most likely more senior than you.

You can help ensure your feedback is received in the spirit in which you are giving it by following some guidelines. Your sponsor is more likely to take your comments well if they are

- Made in private
- Honest and respectful
- Nonjudgmental
- Stated in simple terms
- Provided in manageable portions
- Relevant and appropriate at the time.

What else can you do?

- Begin by setting the scene. Explain the problem and its impacts on the project.

- Always focus on the problem or specific actions, not the person. Try to make the conversation a joint exploration of the problem, which is typically much easier for the recipient to accept.

- Remember to use open-ended questions, listen actively, and avoid "you should" statements.

The following dialogue illustrates how following these pointers can help you, the project manager, deliver feedback that is clear, specific, and sensitive and leads to a productive conversation and solution to the problem:

PM: Do you have a minute to talk about the email you sent the team the other day?

Sponsor: Sure, I can spare a minute. What's up?

PM: I'm afraid the point of the email was lost on the team.

Sponsor: How do you mean?

PM: Well, I know from our conversations that your intent was to highlight the benefit of our project to the organization, but this was lost in some of the details of the message.

Sponsor: I'm not sure I understand.

PM: You did a great job of highlighting the benefits, but the team took the recap of some of the project issues as criticism of their work. The water cooler conversation I heard after had hints of "Doesn't she know what we have to deal with?"

Sponsor: But I do know with what they are dealing with. I have been working to remove some of the barriers that have impacted the project.

PM: I understand that, but it didn't come across in the message and they don't know what you're doing like I do. I've tried to talk to them about some of our conversations and planned actions. But I'm losing credibility with them.

Sponsor: Oh, I didn't even think about the context in which they would receive the message. What can I do to help?

PM: I think two things would help. Acknowledging the issues and the work the team has done to attempt to resolve them would be helpful. Also, if they had some evidence of what you are doing to aid in the matter, they would see that you are supporting the project, not judging.

Sponsor: That makes sense. Please schedule some time with my assistant that I can drop into one of your team meetings and talk more about these issues. This will be a great opportunity for me to hear their thoughts on the causes and potential resolutions as well. Do you think that will help?

PM: Yes, that would be perfect! Thank you. I'll make sure to get an agenda with the objectives of your joining us so that they immediately know we have a plan to inform and involve them.

Here are a few more simple rules you can follow when giving feedback:

- **Focus your feedback.** For feedback to be really meaningful, it must be very specific. For example, you might say, "When you briefed the project team, they were clearly left confused about the purpose of the project."

- **Form an observation rather than inferences.** Stated another way, **be descriptive, not judgmental.** Avoid trying to interpret the sponsor's actions. Explain what you're seeing exactly as it appears. For instance, you could say: "On three occasions you have spoken with the project team and given them specific tasks to do. I wonder how aware you are about how that makes me feel." This is far more effective than saying "You have completely undermined my position by your actions."

- **Request ideas, rather than giving advice.** By sharing information, you allow the sponsor to come to her own conclusions about what she needs to do. You might say, "It looks like Accounts want more input into this project. What do you think?" **Feedback is better received when solicited rather than imposed.** Whenever possible, ask the sponsor if she "would like some feedback on . . . ." People are often starved for feedback, and that includes project sponsors.

> **MAKING RECOMMENDATIONS**
>
> We suggest the following five steps when making a recommendation to your project sponsor:
>
> 1. Clearly state the problem or opportunity.
> 2. Explain the impacts of the current state on the project.
> 3. Make your recommendation.
> 4. Describe the expected benefits to the project.
> 5. Provide alternatives with expected impacts.
>
> Here's how a conversation according to these steps between a project manager and sponsor might go:
>
> *PM:* I am having a problem with the project team that I could really use your help with.
>
> *Sponsor:* What is it? I'd love to help if I can.
>
> *PM:* Well, I am hearing grumblings that they do not think their work on the project is valued. I feel I have done everything within my control that I can to show how I appreciate them and the work they do.
>
> *Sponsor:* Seems like that should be enough.

PM: Apparently not. They continue to show signs of not being motivated and I have heard them say on occasion that management doesn't seem to care.

Sponsor: What can I do to help?

PM: I think it would be helpful if there were some public way you could acknowledge the team and demonstrate how the work they are doing is contributing to the organization's objectives. Do you have any thoughts on how to accomplish this?

Sponsor: I could drop by the project area and give a pep talk.

PM: That would help, but we'd need to be careful that it comes across as sincere and not just blowing smoke. I would know that was not your intention, but they are very sensitive and pessimistic right now.

Sponsor: I'd be open to your ideas on how to craft the message. I could also contribute an article about the project to our employee newsletter.

PM: That would be wonderful. What if we do the article and then plan a quick celebration with the team to discuss?

Sponsor: Yes, I can see how that would help. I'll try to get on that as soon as I can.

PM: What can I do to help?

Sponsor: Actually, if you can draft an article and send it to me to review, I can make edits and submit it to the communications department. That would be a big help. Also, work with my assistant to find an hour on my calendar in about two weeks.

PM: Excellent! I am more than happy to help get this moving. Please let me know if there is anything else I can do.

DELIVERING BAD NEWS

There may be also be times when you have to deliver bad news to your sponsor. Someone is leaving the project, the tests of the prototype have gone badly wrong, there is a delay in the project, costs are up, progress is down, something is amiss somewhere. Bad news is the news of the day. It is imperative that you deliver this news as soon as possible to retain the sponsor's trust. The worst case for you and the project is that she learns of the bad news some other way. You risk losing credibility and trust, and also run the risk of the project sponsor coming in to play hero without the full context of firsthand news. Here are some tips to keep in mind:

- **Deliver the news in person if at all possible.** Sometimes, in this modern world of virtual projects that span the globe, project managers have no choice but to share bad news by other means, such as by phone. But avoid panicky exclamations—"The project has stopped! We are all doomed!" as well as inappropriate means of communication, like a text message saying "Project costs up 150%. Sorry ☹."

- **Deliver the news in the right place at the right time.** Don't delay, but don't break down by the coffee machine and tell your sponsor that half of the project team has quit. Set up a meeting and let the sponsor know, if possible, that this is not just a regular update but an issue you need her help with. For example, tell her "I want to brief you on some rumors I am hearing about our competition."

- **Deliver the news with some ideas for recovery.** We all want to hear solutions, not just problems, and sponsors are no different. A problem without a solution is a complaint and the person delivering it a complainer. Come to the news-sharing meeting ready at least with some ideas for addressing the problem. If you can't come up with any solutions, at least prepare a statement of impact and some suggestions for thinking through solution or response options. For instance: "Since the tests have failed so badly, could we meet with the key players to talk through some ways forward?"

Keep in mind the difference between symptoms and actual problems. Do some digging in advance about the root causes of the problem. You may need to recommend remedial actions to address the symptoms, but don't discount addressing the cause. If you do, you'll likely end up facing a bad news day again.

- **Be ready to follow up.** Once the news is out, action is required, and you will need to be ready to take the actions you've agreed on with your sponsor to get this project back on the road. Follow the "plan-do-check-act" or Deming cycle shown in Figure 2-1 to validate that the problem is getting resolution:
    o **Plan** the steps discussed to correct the issue.
    o **Do** the activity.
    o **Check** that the actions have created the expected results.
    o **Act** to adjust the plan as needed improve results as needed.

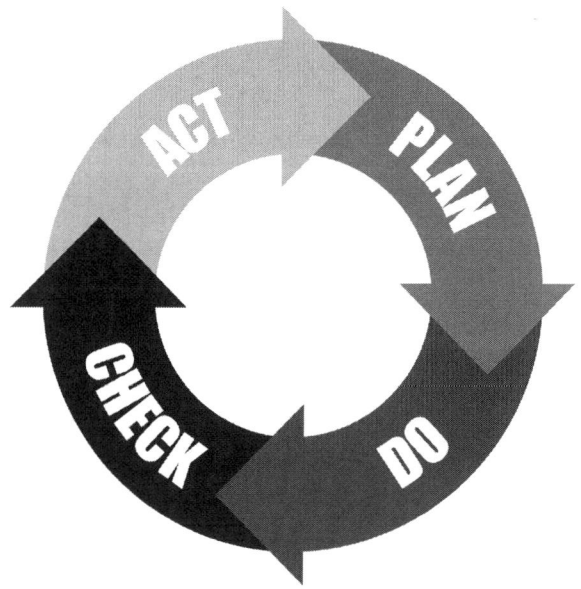

FIGURE 2-1: The Deming "Plan-Do-Check-Act" Cycle

COACHING YOUR SPONSOR

What having a personal trainer is for your body, having a coach can be for your mind. In a later chapter, we explore the kinds of training that work and don't work with sponsors; for now, let's just accept that you, as project manager, may need to step in when training is needed—and has proven inadequate or unavailable.

You will be a coach. You will be a sounding board, a support system, a cheerleader, and a buddy all rolled into one. It's no simple job, and since you will also be managing a project or two, you will be doing it in your spare time. You can begin by understanding why your sponsor might require coaching.

People seek coaches for many reasons, including personal, professional, or some combination of the two. They may wish to find a balance between their personal and professional lives or to become more productive or effective.

Coaching your sponsor can help her become more productive in her work—specifically her duties on your project. Perhaps she has come to her own conclusion, or you have convinced her, that she needs help to become a better sponsor and to have a better understanding of the project management world. Remember, those in leadership roles strive to be the best at what they do. Use this to inspire and motivate your sponsor to accept your coaching. Choose your words and tone carefully so that you come across as helpful, not patronizing or condescending, to build camaraderie.

You could coach her on basic project matters, but it might be best to leave this to outside professionals if you can convince your sponsor and company to invest in it. Letting others provide this kind of coaching will save you time. But if this isn't a possibility, it will be up to you to act as coach.

If she is open to coaching, you can openly offer information and opinions. Give her a copy of this book, send her articles, and talk to her about formal project management, best practices, and how she can help the project succeed. Spend more time reviewing project plans with her to highlight the advantages of project management best practices and specific actions she can take to optimize the chances of success.

If your sponsor is resistant to coaching, you will need to provide the information in a subtle way, in context and when issues arise, using strategies that will be discussed later in this chapter. Remember that when coaching is done really well, people may not even realize they are being coached!

THE SPONSOR RESPONSIBILITIES EVALUATION TOOL

What is clear is that there is no consensus among the professional organizations about the role of the project sponsor. It falls to us, as project managers, to ensure not only that the role is clearly defined but also that both managers and sponsors fully understand what the role involves.

We, the authors, believe that a simple checklist can help in clarifying what the sponsor role is and is not. We present in this book several sponsor responsibilities checklist-based tools for sponsors and project managers to use in defining, communicating, and carrying out their roles.

Checklists are useful in many areas. They act as a reminder to the individual user and provide a way to communicate to team members the tasks yet to be done. The following story may convince even skeptics that checklists can be critically important to a project.[1]

In October 1935, the U.S. Army Air Corps held a flight competition for airplane manufacturers vying to build the army's next-generation long-range bomber. The overwhelming favorite going into the contest was the Boeing Model 299, which was dubbed "the flying fortress." It carried five times as many bombs as the army requested and flew almost twice as far.

But disaster struck; the plane crashed, killing two members of the flight crew, including the pilot, Major P. P. Hill.

An investigation revealed that nothing mechanical had gone wrong. The crash was attributed to pilot error. The report suggested that the 299 was too much aircraft for one man to fly.

Boeing decided to follow up. They gathered a few test pilots to evaluate the situation and see what they could come up with.

The pilot was highly experienced, so general training was not the issue. But in looking back at the accident report, the pilots found that Hill was unfamiliar with the aircraft and had neglected to release the elevator lock prior to takeoff. Once the plane was airborne, the Boeing chief test pilot realized what was happening and tried to reach the lock handle, but it was too late.

The pilots saw that they needed some way of making sure that everything necessary was done before takeoff. What resulted was a series of checklists for pilots: one for takeoff, one for flight, one for before landing, and one for after landing. In a sense, it was true that the 299 was too much for one man to fly: it was simply too complex for any one person's memory. But these checklists for the pilot and copilot made sure that nothing was forgotten or overlooked.

Thanks to the checklists, careful planning, and rigorous training, the 12 planes the army initially ordered flew 1.8 million miles without a serious accident. The army then accepted the 299 and eventually ordered 12,731 of the aircraft they numbered the B-17.

And so the checklist was born.

Sponsorship is often not as strong a role as it should be. For example, we found that 74 percent of sponsors receive no training, and 21 percent of sponsors have little or no impact on the projects they sponsor (see Appendix A). Weak sponsorship probably hasn't led to any plane crashes—as far as we know—but sufficient evidence exists to say that sponsorship surely could and should be better. We concluded that the role needs a definitive checklist of responsibilities to help sponsors focus on stronger sponsorship—strength that can be demonstrated by improved survey scores for those who embrace it.

Based on a comprehensive list of sponsor responsibilities we developed (see Appendix B), we present a tool to determine levels of competency and to prioritize strategies for improvement (Figure 2-2). This checklist was designed to help evaluate a sponsor's ability or abilities to carry out the responsibilities of the role. Similar to the flight checklists described above, this checklist can be used before or during the project, during the project closure process, and after the project (for postproject review, lessons learned, or a retrospective).

As a project manager, you can use the checklist to see how well your sponsor is supporting your project or to seek support from a newly assigned sponsor. But if you are a sponsor, you can use the checklist to evaluate yourself. We suggest you give the checklist to others to evaluate you as well. Maybe you do not know yourself as well as others do!

	Sponsor Responsibility	Great	Good	Needs Improvement	Trouble
1	Provides direction and guidance for strategies and initiatives				
2	Works with the project manager to develop the project charter				
3	Identifies and quantifies business benefits to be achieved by successful implementation of the project				
4	Makes go/no-go decisions				
5	Evaluates the project's success upon completion				
6	Negotiates funding for the project				
7	Actively participates in the initial project planning				
8	Reviews and approves changes to plans, priorities, deliverables, schedule, and more				
9	Identifies project steering committee members				
10	Gains agreement among stakeholders when differences of opinion occur				
11	Chairs the project steering committee				
12	Assists the project when required (especially in an out-of-control situation) by exerting organizational authority and the ability to influence				
13	Helps resolve interproject boundary issues				
14	Supports the project manager in conflict resolution				

Sponsor Responsibility		Great	Good	Needs Improvement	Trouble
15	Advises the project manager of protocols, political issues, and potential sensitivities				
16	Makes the project visible within the organization				
17	Encourages stakeholder involvement and builds and maintains their ongoing commitment through effective communication strategies				

FIGURE 2-2: Sponsor Responsibilities Evaluation Tool

To use the checklist, place a check for each competency in the column that corresponds to the appropriate evaluation:

- **Great: the sponsor understands the responsibility and does it well.** Congratulations! You should have an easy time getting this kind of support from your sponsor. Thank her and recognize the good she is doing for the project.

- **Good: the sponsor generally understands the task and does it somewhat well.** Not so bad. You may want to explain how additional support in this area will improve the project and offer specific guidance on tools or techniques she can use. Base your suggestions on your experience and interactions with the project team and stakeholders. Present your advice as a different perspective on how to perform the task, not as a judgment of her ability.

- **Needs improvement: the sponsor does not understand or perform the task.** Your sponsor may not be aware of the task, or perhaps performing the task did not really benefit past projects she has worked on. Work with your sponsor to help her understand the specific outcomes and benefits to the project you would expect to see if she did perform the task. Focus on the best interest of the project, try to understand the sponsor's perspective, and be empathetic to the stressors she is facing. Offer additional information on best practices, using specific examples from your own experience where you can.

- **Trouble: the sponsor does not agree that the task is part of her role.** You may be out of luck here. You can attempt to educate her on the benefits of the task based on your experience, but also consider or discuss other factors that may be influencing her lack of engagement. Keep the focus on the goals of the project and your mutual interest in success. Alternatively, look for other strategies to meet this project need. Is there another active stakeholder who can provide assistance, or can you as the project manager fill the gap?

How did your sponsor score on each competency item?

Do not treat each of these competencies with the same weight of priority. Focus on those that have the biggest impact on risk to the project first and work down from there. Some of these competencies may be adequately handled by other people or in other ways, and that is OK.

SHARING THE PROJECT PASSION WITH YOUR SPONSOR

Something magical happens when you put a group of people who have a shared passion in the same room. We're not just talking excitement here—we are talking passion.

As a project manager, you should have that passion for what you do, and one of your top duties in working with a new project sponsor is to fire her up with the same passion. If she has no project experience, she may not have a clue as to why you do what you do and what is so great about it.

How can you share the passion?

- Discuss the current state and expected end state—what the world will look like once the project is done—and the specific improvements that will be realized as a result.

- Involve her in some of the more fun project activities such as the project kickoff or team celebrations.

- Share some of your past successes, how these made you and your previous sponsors feel, and how they benefitted the organization.

- Tell her about what you have learned in your project management career, the epiphanies you have had, and how these will contribute to the success of the current project.

PLANNING FOR A SPONSOR'S SUDDEN ABSENCE

What would happen if your project sponsor stopped, well, sponsoring? One way to think about this is to consider your sponsor's hypothetical disappearance as if it were a change request. What do you do when a change request comes in, apart from acknowledging it and registering it? You (and your team) assess the change impact and make recommendations accordingly, and assuming the change is approved, you adjust your plan and budget accordingly. Similarly, there would be specific consequences if your sponsor walked away. What are they, and how would you deal with them?

You should draft a change request regarding the possibility that your sponsor will drop out of sight as part of your risk plan if you believe that your project sponsor is in fact a risk. She may be a negative risk in the sense that she is not (yet) the perfect sponsor, or a positive risk because she is an excellent project sponsor but could, perhaps, be called away to attend to a more critical activity.

Let's take a moment to think about how a change request about a missing sponsor might read:

CR #: 911

Title: Loss of Sponsor

Impact: Loss of executive-level support, potential loss of funding

Change request: Appointment of new sponsor

Impact on project:

- Time needed to educate the new sponsor on current project plans and progress
- Potential changes to scope or plans based on the new sponsor's preferences

Other alternatives identified:

- *Continue without sponsor:* The project will probably die a slow death or deliver something that nobody uses.
- *Cancel the project:* No additional investment will be made in the project (this may be the right option if this project is not of sufficient value to be sponsored by someone with the appropriate level of authority). Cancelling will give the impression that money spent so far was wasted, but sunk costs are sunk, so why spend even more if it will not yield value?

We hope that you never need to submit this change request. With this proactive analysis, you reduce the likelihood of needing to cancel a project, because you can leverage the results of the analysis as a means to gain support before the need becomes a reality.

THE PROJECT MANAGER EVALUATION TOOL

Are you the best project manager you can be for your sponsor and project? You have the best of intentions, to be sure, but some objective analysis of your actions can help you figure out what effects they are having.

Review the checklist in Figure 2-3 (see Appendix C for the basic list) and rate how well you are fulfilling the listed tasks and competencies on your current project on a scale of one (weak performance) to five (strong performance). Even better, review this list with your project sponsor. Her input will help you determine what she really needs from you.

Did you score a one or two on any items? Could your weaker performance in those areas be putting the project at risk? If so, what are the specific risks? What can you do to improve your scores? Work to build your competence through training, practice, or with the help of a mentor. In the meantime, perhaps someone on the project team excels naturally in the areas you do not. Consider delegating tasks to him or her.

Project Manager Responsibility	Score (1–5)
Fully briefs project sponsors, stakeholders, and, if appropriate, the project team	
Coaches and advises the project sponsor of project needs	
Proactively monitors and reports delivery of project against key deliverables	
Is ultimately accountable for the project processes and team	
Provides adequate background, analysis, and recommendations to support needed decisions	
Where appropriate, staffs the steering committee (project board); arranges for the committee's administrative needs to be met directly or through delegation	
Provides timely and sufficient information about potential resource needs	
Fully understands the organization's strategy and how projects fit into it	
Provides project documentation that informs the sponsor and stakeholders of project plans and status	
Monitors and tracks the change management process, bringing necessary items to the project sponsor's or steering committee's (project board's) attention	
Keeps the sponsor informed on budget and schedule tracking; alerts her early of potential shortfalls and offers recommendations to respond or adjust	
Understands project status at all times and how it fits with the organization's project status as well as the overall project management approach used internally	
Demonstrates strong leadership throughout the project	
Promotes partnership/collaborative working across the organization and externally	
Networks effectively and brokers good relationships with stakeholders	
Is able to demonstrate effective communication in all areas	
Fully understands project management and its implications for project success	
Fully understands the project management life cycle model and can guide others in its use	
Responds to notice of protocols, political issues, and potential sensitivities by actively tracking risks (including mitigation and contingency strategies) and issues	
Provides information to the sponsor on project barriers with context, background, and recommended actions	

FIGURE 2-3: Project Manager Evaluation Tool

Where did you score fours and fives? How can you exploit these competencies for the betterment of the project? The evaluation tool can be used by the project team as well. Though the project team is not the overall focus for this book, the project team can use it to help and support the project manager, which clearly supports the project sponsor. Additionally, it could help the overall development process by bringing forward an individual capable of suggesting to them the wider picture. We do not recommend you try to score a five on every item, only that you consider each activity and its direct contribution to your current project and work on those duties that will have the greatest impact on the project.

NOTES

1 Atul Gawande, "The Checklist," *The New Yorker* (December 10, 2007).

CHAPTER 3
Working with Challenging Sponsors

You will not get the perfect project sponsor, and you shouldn't expect to. The reality, which is also true of every team member and every other stakeholder—and of you, if you are completely honest—is that you will get what you get, and you will have to adapt your style, approach, and management technique accordingly.

Think of working with a sponsor in the same terms as you might your project team. It is a truly lucky project manager who gets exactly the project team that he wants; the likelihood is that what you get will be a compromise of some sort. You wanted Jill, but she wasn't available at the time, and so you got Jack . . . but he is less skilled than Jill, and so you also get some of John's time, and so on. You will have to make the most of that team, and you'll have to do the same with your sponsor. You will have to compensate for any gaps in her skills and authority, and you should aim to maximize the positive elements she brings to the project.

To be fair, not all the project problems you face will be caused by the sponsor. Nevertheless, the purpose of this chapter is to explore the ways you can manage the many "types" of challenging project sponsor you may encounter throughout your project management career. Each type can challenge the project in unique ways:

- The absent sponsor
- The busy sponsor
- The uninterested sponsor
- The inexperienced sponsor
- The sponsor who wants to be the project manager
- The sponsor who gets involved too late
- The untrained sponsor
- The sponsor who is part of a committee of sponsors
- The saboteur or just plain bad sponsor.

In presenting our analysis, we've drawn an analogy to medical diagnosis. To help you identify and "treat" project difficulties brought on by inadequate sponsorship, we list for each type the symptoms you may see in your project and the prognosis for afflicted projects if the causes are left untreated. We also prescribe the actions that will be needed to bring a project back to health.

As part of the research for this book, we sent out a worldwide call for sponsor stories through our individual and collective social media networks. We present some of these stories as "case notes," along with stories based on our experiences over the years.

THE ABSENT SPONSOR

Symptoms
- There is not an assigned project sponsor.
- There is a sponsor assigned but you have never met with her.
- You have an assigned sponsor who frequently misses or cancels meetings.

Prognosis Challenged Project!
- The project manager invests far more time than is expected because he needs to fill two roles.
- The business is not represented in an objective manner with regard to the project.
- The project manager may make decisions outside their authority range.
- There is a lack of progress in starting the project, moving the project through the various phases. Getting agreement on the project scope may well be difficult to obtain and if it is agreed, it's a slow and difficult process.
- The project team, including the project manager, feels the project is not important and loses motivation.
- It is difficult to keep the project on schedule as there is no executive support to mitigate risk, break down barriers, or demonstrate priority.

Prescription Figure out what type of absent sponsor you are dealing with by finding the root cause:
- Is she just too busy with other, more pressing demands on her time? In that case, see the section on the busy sponsor.
- Has she disappeared because she doesn't know how to contribute to the project or behave as a project sponsor? See the section on the untrained sponsor.
- Is the problem that she doesn't believe in the project (perhaps even expects or wants it to fail) and therefore doesn't want to appear to be associated with it in any way? In this case, replacing the sponsor can be an option, but this will require the involvement of a higher authority who understands the problem and can function as an arbitrator in the replacement of the sponsor.
- Was she supportive and involved originally but no longer has a vested interest in the project as a result of restructuring or realignment of accountabilities? In this case, too, you need to seek out an alternative sponsor.

CASE NOTES: 1

A major bank in Switzerland embarked on a risk management program. It was a challenging program to implement; one of the problems it was supposed to solve was that at that time, the bank did not have an email or groupware system that allowed attachments, so everything had to be mailed.

Initially, there was a real lack of progress on the project, and the first project manager left the project. Why? Because the project could not attract a sponsor.

When the second project manager took over, he conducted a full review due to concerns that the project could not be delivered. He requested that the budget be more than doubled, which would allow the program to go global, not just cover a few countries. However, every time the new project manager attempted to get approval for the budget, the committee asked the new project manager to go away to get more and more information, never making a decision.

Eventually, the project manager provided the committee with evidence that the bank would save a large amount of money per month by implementing the new system. But still there was no agreement.

The project manager asked the committee, "Who wants to continue to delay the decision about this email system, thereby losing the bank this [previously declared to be significant] amount per month?" No one responded, so it was decided that the program had passed. The chief information officer (CIO) stood up and said that the project manager's presentation was excellent and that he would act as sponsor moving forward. He hadn't felt comfortable standing up for the project before consensus was reached, but once it was gained he was more than willing to be the sponsor.

The process just to get the budget for the project approved took six months; actually performing the project for 15 countries took nine months. In the end, the project was a success in every sense and was the bank's first successful global initiative.

CASE NOTES: 2

I was contracted to work on a project that was mandated by the U.S. government to collect data across jurisdictions. I was given two sponsors' names. One was the CIO, the other the director of the division responsible for the data. I briefly met the CIO in passing early on but was having problems getting information on or from the division director. He was located in another building, so proximity was working against me.

I began to arrange a kickoff meeting where I would review the project objectives and scope with all stakeholders, including the two sponsors. I managed to get them both scheduled for the event and thought it was a go. I was told by my contract manager (a direct report of the CIO) to cancel the meeting two days before because "we" were not ready. The meeting never came to be.

As the project progressed, I became aware of which stakeholder, a unit manager, had the greatest interest in and influence over the project. This was the person I needed to be the closest to in order to effectively lead the project in the direction intended. The manager was not a named sponsor, but he had the largest interest and stake in the project and was in the best position to be the project sponsor.

A result of the lack of an appropriately named sponsor was chaos. It was impossible to nail down the scope of work for the project. I reported through the technical side of the house, and its definition of project success was not aligned with the business purpose for the project. The technical people wanted to solve all of their technical issues, not focus on the federal data mandates as intended. Scope decisions were discussed over and over with no consensus on what was truly needed. Changes to decisions were daily events, and the unit manager who would have been a better fit as sponsor was brought into discussions only when he demanded information. The CIO's staff was running the show.

The lesson I learned was that it is essential to develop a close relationship and rapport with the person who best meets the definition of sponsor, regardless of who the official sponsor is. I realized that I needed to discover as early as possible who this person was, because he or she would be in the best position to have a positive (or even negative) impact on the project. Working together, we could have much more effectively solidified the project scope and goals. Perhaps we could have gotten formal direction from the sponsor, his boss, about delegation or even an official charter change.

I included a recommendation in my postproject report that the organization review the project governance structure to assign sponsors who had the necessary interest in and influence on the project and not rely on the organization governance structure to dictate sponsors.

Swapping sponsors midproject requires convincing *two* people of the benefits to them and the project if the switch is made. First, you have to get the existing sponsor to agree to relinquish the role. Some will have no problem with this, but in other cases, the idea will need to be carefully broached to ensure that the sponsor understands that the switch is being made for the greater good of the project and business and is not an indictment of her capability. Then, of course, you'll need to convince the new would-be sponsor that this is her opportunity to get on board and that becoming the sponsor for this project will benefit not only the project and business but her, too.

It is possible that the project management office (PMO)[1] could help by acting as a sort of interim sponsor if no other alternative is possible. Failure to deal with the absent sponsor will mean that the project manager will end up doing the job of two people—and that is neither easy nor desirable.

THE BUSY SPONSOR

Symptoms
- No access to assigned sponsor
- Project does not get sponsor's attention due to competing priorities
- Missed or rescheduled meetings

Prognosis Challenged Project!
- Delays in significant decision-making and/or support activities affect project progress and waste the project team's time.
- The team feels disconnected from executive support and guidance.
- Team members may question the importance of the project and may reduce their efforts accordingly.
- Stakeholders do not give priority to project needs.

Prescription
- Every project needs a business case—the foundation of the project. It should be signed off by the project sponsor. This is your opportunity to engage with the sponsor face-to-face. The importance of the business case cannot be overstated, and getting the sponsor's signature is your opportunity to discuss with her what the project entails, the likely resources needed, and her role. Ultimately, if she does not sign off on the business case, you have no project and the work stops.
- Secure indirect access to the sponsor through her personal assistant or deputy or another stakeholder with high influence and high interest.
- Identify what it is that is taking her time and how she came to sponsor your project if she is so busy.

- Try getting the sponsor to agree to a very short (even ten-minute) meeting to start with. Explain that you recognize she is a busy/important person and want to find the best way of working with her without distracting her too much.
  - Prepare for that meeting with succinct points: this is what a sponsor should do (responsibilities); this is how much time is needed, etc.
  - Ask the key question: can she commit to this project? If she can't, explain the risk of her absence to the project and consider a plan B. Is there someone else who could deputize for the busy sponsor or even take over the role?
  - What is of interest to her about this project—does she care about it? If she does, she has to start engaging with you to make sure the project gets sufficient time and support. If she doesn't care, it is time to try to find an alternative sponsor.
- Add to the risk register the impact the sponsor's lack of involvement is having on the project and share it with her (if only by email). You are going out on a limb here—this is dangerous if you do and dangerous if you don't!

CASE NOTES

When I began managing a project in a health organization, I tried to be a responsible project manager by asking who the sponsor was and when I could meet her. I was told that for this project, the sponsor would be the director of patient care, but she was busy right now and would get back to me as soon as she could. Resources were already scheduled to start the project, so we got on with it anyway.

Despite many attempts to get access to and time with the sponsor, her schedule of meetings (apparently back to back, almost 24/7) did not allow any such face time (or, in fact, any remote time either). Finally, I got a meeting scheduled some two months after the project started, just in time to show a prototype of the solution we were developing.

Sure enough, the sponsor arrived—late—at the meeting. This was not a one-on-one session, but a group gathering where we were demonstrating what we planned to deliver to the health organization eventually. We clearly explained that the data that we were about to show were not 100 percent accurate and that the focus of the presentation was the reporting system, not the data itself.

In the middle of the demonstration, the sponsor stopped the presentation, asked several questions about one element of the data, and then leapt up, saying that she was going to talk to the head of the relevant department now about the stats. And she left.

The next time we met was when the project had completed and we were wrapping things up.

THE UNINTERESTED SPONSOR

Symptoms
- Assigned sponsor scores low on the Power Grid (Chapter 1)
- Sponsor does not take an ownership or authoritative voice in discussing the project (may refer to it the company's or someone else's project)
- Sponsor defers important decisions to others
- Project does not get sponsor's attention due to competing priorities
- Missed or rescheduled meetings

Prognosis   Challenged Project!
- The project manager invests far more time than is expected because he needs to fill two roles.
- The key stakeholders (different parts of the business) are not represented. This means their views cannot and will not be taken into account. Decisions will be made but without the engagement or participation of the key stakeholders. The project slows down and loses direction and impetus as a result of the absence of appropriate authority. In fact, if the sponsor has no interest from the very start of the project, it may never even get off the ground.

- Decision-making can be very difficult. Project managers usually know what decisions they can make—generally decisions that are in line with the company's overall governance processes. But if the project manager is acting as a surrogate sponsor, he may be faced with decisions about, for example, spending and resource allocation that he doesn't have the authority to make.

Prescription   As with the absent sponsor, first you need to determine what type of uninterested sponsor you are dealing with. It is important to get to the root of why she doesn't seem to care:

- Does she seem uninterested only because she doesn't know how to contribute to the project or behave as a project sponsor? See the section on the untrained sponsor.
- Is the problem that she doesn't believe in the project (perhaps even expects or wants it to fail) and therefore doesn't want to appear to be associated with it in any way?

Once you have done that, you may be able to work with her to help her raise her game for the duration of the project, at least. Perhaps it is time to have a direct one-on-one with the sponsor. If she is willing to give you time for meetings, then access will not be the issue. In the meeting, you should

- Speak honestly about the issues that you are facing and the challenges your project is dealing with as a consequence of her lack of interest.
- Discuss what executive management expects from project sponsors and how not being fully engaged in the project will affect her personally.

Go back to the business case and see what is in it for her. Did she have concerns at the start about the business case? Was she overruled by other executives (and then forced to sponsor something she didn't believe in)? What were her concerns, and can any changes be made now to address them? The bottom line is that you must work with her to try to get to the bottom of her behavior.

CASE NOTES

The sponsor on my project just doesn't seem to care about the project at all. She agrees to meetings with no problem, so it's not as if she doesn't have time. But when we're meeting, she just goes through the motions, and as soon as the meeting is over, she doesn't do anything else on the project. It almost seems as if it's a relief for her to escape and go back to other matters of work.

The project is struggling to get a real foothold in the organization, and I have lost a couple of key resources already to more "glamorous" projects.

THE INEXPERIENCED SPONSOR

Symptoms
- First assignment as project sponsor
- No prior experience in projects as a team member or key stakeholder
- Lack of awareness of the project best practices and the project life cycle

Prognosis Challenged Project!
- The project manager has to spend even more time than usual on the project because he must answer the sponsor's questions about what should be done and why. He has less time for the project team and for communicating with others.
- All decisions have to go through the project manager because the sponsor doesn't know what to do, creating a bottleneck that delays progress.

Prescription The inexperienced sponsor will either
- Do nothing about her inexperience, thereby putting the burden of both roles on the project manager, or
- Have a desire to learn. This burdens the project manager by adding a coaching element to his role (assuming the organization doesn't have an in-house or third-party sponsor development program; see the section on the untrained sponsor), beyond the burden the project manager bears during the initial part of the project to also act as the sponsor.

If the former is true, then apply the aforementioned guidance for working with an absent sponsor.

If the latter is true, since the sponsor is keen to learn, tell her that you are happy to guide her, but her lack of experience is affecting the project. Options then are to arrange some kind of training (see the section on the untrained sponsor), to have a more experienced sponsor in the company coach her, or to accept that you are the best person to help her. This will, of course, add work to the project plan, so you will have to revise the plan to build in the added effort.

It is possible that the PMO could help by acting as a sort of interim sponsor if no other alternative is possible.

CASE NOTES

I spend most of my time with my project sponsor. Well, I *say* sponsor, but in reality she is just a figurehead right now. Enthusiastic for sure, but this is her first-ever project—she has never even managed one—and she has no idea what she is supposed to be doing most of the time. But she's on the fast track within our company, and this is something that she has to learn on the way to the top, I guess. Guiding her is just hard work, on top of the real project work.

THE SPONSOR WHO WANTS TO BE THE PROJECT MANAGER

Symptoms
- The project sponsor is eager to micromanage the project itself, testing and checking everything that the actual project manager does.
- Project management decisions are often revisited and overturned.
- The sponsor is driving project tasks rather than the project manager.

Prognosis Challenged Project!
- The project manager is increasingly frustrated by this level of detailed management and rebels against it by trying to avoid the project sponsor as much as possible.
- Project progress is hindered by a double layer of reporting, validation, and clarification.
- The project manager becomes disengaged and demotivated.
- Project team members are unsure about reporting channels or escalation channels, since the project sponsor and the project manager appear to be one and the same.
- Creativity shrivels and dies when a sponsor starts getting involved in team decisions and directing individual work. When you hear team members say things like, "If the sponsor wanted it that way, why doesn't she just do it herself?" it's time to evaluate your sponsor's level of involvement.

Prescription Go back to basics when dealing with a micromanaging sponsor:
- Show your sponsor the project sponsor tasks in the project life cycle[2] to reinforce what she really should be concentrating on. Reiterate that this is her role, and reconfirm your own responsibilities in your role as project manager.

- Give her specific examples of the negative effects that her over involvement is having on the project. Track her decisions (and changes she's made to decisions) with real impacts (in time and dollars) to highlight the overall impact.

Once you've talked with the sponsor, you need to understand why she is micromanaging you. What do you know about her? Is she behaving this way because of a bad previous experience? Is she under extreme pressure to deliver? The more you understand, the better you can deal with the situation.

If you have managed a project before (assuming it wasn't a disaster, of course), perhaps get the sponsor for that project to have a word with your current sponsor. This might allay any concerns that she has about your competence and ability.

Always emphasize that you have the same interest in project success and want to build a relationship that supports both of your needs toward this end.

CASE NOTES: 1

The project was challenging (seemingly close to impossible at times); the steering committee was difficult to work with (to say the least); the project sponsor was everywhere, always in a bad micromanaging sort of way; the project team members' interest and capability varied (to put it mildly); and I was a long way from home. From day one, the entire experience really tested me as a project manager, but I felt that I had conducted myself well—until the very end of the project, that is.

Finally the project reached its conclusion. The deliverables were delivered and the company reluctantly agreed to sign off on the project. I had had quite a hellish experience over the months and just wanted it all to come to an end. And so when that final steering committee meeting was over and the minutes signed off, I have to admit that I practically ran to my car, jumped in, and tore out of the parking lot deliriously happy. The road home called to me and, with some rock music blaring out of the speakers, I decided to write this one off to history and to never return again. The job was done!

Except that it wasn't. I was asked to go back and do a post project review.

My heart sank, and I began to make up 101 reasons why I was too busy, too sick, too mentally incompetent, too "about to go on a spontaneous holiday," and too "I just don't want to go back," in order to, well, avoid going back.

I didn't go back. Someone else did. And so that was that.

Except it wasn't. My inquisitiveness eventually got the better of me, so I sat down with the other project manager sometime after the review, and I discovered many things that I had never known about my own project.

I learned that the company and the project sponsor had had a very bad experience on a similar project and, as a result, they were nervous about this project, very nervous indeed. The previous project was still going on and still costing money and not delivering.

I discovered that the project I'd managed had been strongly championed by the project sponsor despite a lot of resistance from others in the business, and a lot—the sponsor's reputation and possibly career—depended on a successful outcome.

CASE NOTES: 2

Early in my career, I worked on a project where the sponsor (to whom I directly reported) was an intense micromanager. The sponsor's personal preferences regarding due dates should have been the first warning sign that he was going to get more and more involved. As the project progressed, I began spending more of my time pulling together materials to keep him informed. It got to the point where he was reviewing work products line by line and I was having hour-long meetings with him morning and afternoon to review project status. Further complicating things was the fact that the sponsor reversed (and re-reversed) decisions that had been made weeks ago because he changed his mind.

It wasn't appropriate for the sponsor to be involved in any of these decisions or work products, but I didn't feel that I had the authority to contradict my direct supervisor. As things unraveled, I sought advice from very senior project managers and tried to explain to the sponsor the risk his actions were placing on the project. Next, a contracted senior project manager told the sponsor to back off—to no avail. The sponsor wanted to do it his way. Team morale plummeted and deadlines slipped.

I learned the valuable lesson that I have to intervene with a micromanaging sponsor much earlier and stick to the roles and responsibilities in the charter from day one.

THE SPONSOR WHO GETS INVOLVED TOO LATE

Symptoms
- Sponsor shows sudden interest in your project.
- Project processes and the team are disrupted.

Prognosis Opportunity!
Yes, the disruption that can be caused by a force can be frustrating. Let's look at the bright side.
- You now have executive-level support of your project.
- You have an opportunity to delegate up for responding to project risks and challenges.
- You have a sounding board and comrade for discussing project decisions.

The project manager's response can turn this change into an opportunity and not a challenge (assuming your sponsor is a reasonable person).

Prescription Empathy. Consider the following story—

For a long time, you hear nothing from the sponsor, probably not since the project began . . . then all of a sudden, she becomes overwhelmingly "interested." In reality, she's bowing to outside pressures—she's about to come under personal scrutiny for the project.

The sponsor has been spooked and reacts in the only way she knows. She has finally been struck by the importance of the project within the organization, and she's panicking. You need to do the following:

- Thank the sponsor for her interest.
- Ask what she needs from you to get up to speed on the project.
- Have a candid discussion on roles and expectations moving forward.
- Set up one or more meetings to respond to her needs, including things you have identified.
- Give her an assignment to get her involved. Is there a risk to be mitigated, a barrier to be broken, or a decision to be made where you can give her a small win as project sponsor?
- Move quickly to build rapport and trust moving forward.

CASE NOTES

When the project sponsor was first appointed, he had a brief flirtation with the project, taking some interest in what deliverables were expected, but nothing heavy—and then he disappeared. Other matters of more importance were taking up his time, so the project manager just got on with it.

Suddenly, with no warning or preparation, the project manager received a call from the sponsor, who was standing outside a meeting of his executive peers. His tone was harsh and aggressive, and he demanded that the project manager confirm that the project was on schedule and that all of the deliverables would be 100 percent as expected. He said that he would hold the project manager personally accountable for any failure. And that was it. Call over.

The project manager was in something of a state of shock and attempted to schedule a meeting with the sponsor to get an understanding of what was going on—why the call now? The sponsor refused to meet. Seven weeks later, the sponsor reengaged with the project by demanding a series of presentations and demonstrations of the deliverables by key team members. The project manager was invited as a guest to those meetings.

In the end, the project delivered to the level that the project manager had first indicated. But the sponsor's additional expectations were never met, and the relationship between him and the project manager was damaged for the long term.

THE UNTRAINED SPONSOR

Symptoms
- Frequently requests changes to process that don't align with project plans
- Requests information or work product that does not provide value to the project
- Confusion or a lack of belief regarding the project initiative and potential benefits
- A feeling of "wait for the next change" infects the project team.

Prognosis Challenged Project!
- The vision and direction of the project or program may become unclear or unstable.
- Changes regarding the project's purpose are forever being presented to stakeholders.
- Progress slows or even halts, since team members have learned that today's change is merely transient and more change will inevitably come.

Prescription A skilled, experienced sponsor would not destabilize a project by constantly changing her mind about its direction. You, as the project manager, should educate her one-on-one and offer guidance. Try to head off further changes by quantifying the value that previous decisions have added to the business, and present this information to the sponsor in an advisory manner.

The classic classroom approach may not be effective with the typical senior manager, so training needs to be provided in a less traditional way. The guidance in Chapter 7, in the "Too Cool for School: Making Sponsorship Training Work" section, may help.

CASE NOTES

The sponsor of the program was a man who believed that he knew everything about everything, because he had been successful in what he had achieved to date. As such he was not a person to take advice well and was not a person who would acknowledge that he needed to learn anything new.

There was a serious problem with some of the supporting systems in our data centers, which this sponsor knew about, but he was not close enough to understand how those systems were really used. People had tried to fix them before, but nothing had resulted.

This time, a major program of investment in the systems was kicked off, and a superb, collaborative program manager brought in. The program team did a really good job of making sense of the whole. They created a vision of a genuinely changed environment. Things really were going to be different this time, since the team realized that working practices needed to change. Even though new systems were being implemented, the program was about business process change more than technical change.

The first project was kicked off, and everyone was fired up about doing things properly this time. Amazingly, it seemed to be working. The project was running on time, and all was going well.

But the sponsor was impatient. More projects were needed, and faster. At steering committee meetings he behaved like an attack dog, and he changed the direction of the program team every month. Each month they were required to spend more and more time producing different analyses of possibilities for the steering committee. At one point, all development work was stopped to divert every possible resource to do analysis for the steering committee.

The program team, however, continued its outreach work. One day, the team was presenting at a project management department briefing session. The message—"business process change more than technical change"—was understood and well received. At the end of the session, the sponsor walked in (he was the next presenter on an unrelated matter). He chipped in with "Rubbish! The program is only about technical change."

Despite all of these issues, the first project delivered. This was an amazing success for the teams involved, but they were not allowed to launch to any fanfare, as the sponsor was about to outsource the whole thing and didn't want any confusing positive messages to get out.

Five years on, and many millions in, the new systems are not being fully used, and the data centers are still relying on the old flaky systems and the old flaky processes.

THE SPONSOR WHO IS PART OF A COMMITTEE OF SPONSORS

Symptoms
- Utter confusion
- Time spent communicating with, negotiating with, and often refereeing multiple parties.

These problems are exacerbated when the sponsors are not "good" project sponsors but rather a mixture of all of the "less than good" characters previously discussed.

Prognosis Challenged Project!
- Project progress may well halt or has already halted.
- The project manager's time is spent dealing with the various sponsors and their interests instead of attending to his other duties.

Prescription   You can try one or more of several approaches to manage or resolve the problem of having too many sponsors:

- The best approach is to interview each sponsor separately to understand her objectives and interest in the project. Alternatively, you can gather the sponsors together for an open discussion. Put the "elephant in the room" topic up for discussion and talk about how best to align these objectives and interests to meet the chartered project outcomes.
- Identify, using the Sponsor Responsibilities Evaluation Tool (Figure 2-2), the strengths and weaknesses of each sponsor.
- Adopt the "one is good, two is OK, but three is a crowd" philosophy and try to reduce the sponsor head count to one or two. Having three or more sponsors generally puts a much higher risk on the project.
- Secure agreement on which sponsor the project manager should work through. This sponsor is then responsible for coordinating the committee's decisions and project review.
- Escalate the problems that have arisen from having too many sponsors through the most significant and appropriate sponsor (that is, the one that you really think is right for the project) up to the executive level.
- Raise and document the problem as a risk to the project if not resolved.

CASE NOTES

An experienced colleague and I once met with a small group of three individuals in a British company. This company was very interested in initiating a business change project and engaged my colleague and me to complete a project readiness assessment.

This assessment was a common service offering that ran over two days and allowed us to consider the readiness of a company for a planned-for project. We would look at the business case, objectives, and planned project deliverables. We would consider risks and constraints. We would assess resources and management support for the project. At the end of the two days of interviews, we'd go away and produce a project success plan outlining the project at a high level and indicating, using a "traffic light" system, any areas of weakness in the proposed project. Red issues required mandatory action before commencing the project, and amber (or orange) issues required action as early as possible in the project life cycle.

On day one, we arrived to interview the three sponsors of the project: the IT manager, the sales and marketing director, and the operations director.

We were greeted by the IT manager, and he laid out the bare bones of the project. This worried us a bit, as it immediately seemed to be an IT-led rather than business-led project, always a challenge. Anyway, we spent two hours with the IT manager, who then introduced us to the operations director.

My colleague outlined everything we knew about the proposed project. Proudly turning to the operations director, confident in his professional style and ability to absorb and present information, he asked if he had missed anything.

"Yes," said the director. "The point!"

It became clear—as the IT manager and the operations director began to argue, quietly at first and then significantly louder—that there was almost no level of agreement between the two. Indeed, it seemed as if they had never even discussed the project before. A red alert on our report was guaranteed.

We were asked to leave the office and wait. We were shown to a small area with a balcony where we could wait and so, on a fresh spring morning, we stared out over the balcony and waited. And waited. And waited some more.

Eventually we decided to head back to see if any common ground had been established, or perhaps one of the combatants had finished the other one off. But nothing. There was no one to be seen, anywhere.

Confused, we managed to find our way back to the reception area and got a call through to the IT manager. Shaken and definitely stirred, he took us to lunch in the café and then pointed us in the direction of the sales and marketing director.

It was my turn to speak, so I stood up, repeated the position and understanding that we'd had up to the start of the meeting with the operations director, and waited—waited for a repeat of the last meeting.

"Looks really good," the sales and marketing director said.

Naturally, we were enormously relieved. We were back on track—or so we thought for about two seconds.

"That said, I don't really care that much," chuckled the sales and marketing director. "I have just handed in my notice—resigned—so I won't be around."

So we went from three project sponsors to none in one morning: one lost because he was leaving (the sales director), one because he had no belief in or support for the proposed project (the operations director), and one because he was just too weak and noncommunicative to act as an effective project sponsor (the IT manager).

In the end, it didn't matter that much. We delivered our report as best we could, but the project was never initiated.[3]

THE SABOTEUR OR JUST PLAIN BAD SPONSOR

Symptoms
- The sponsor operates and behaves in a manner that is the exact opposite of what the project needs her to do if it is to succeed.
- Decisions are frequently revisited and overturned.
- The sponsor refuses to formally accept project deliverables.

Prognosis	Challenged Project! • The sponsor actively challenges the project manager at every step. • The project has become isolated and potentially detached from the business strategy. • The project will suffer delays due to constant changes in direction and tasks. • The reputation of the project manager and the project team may become tainted.
Prescription	Every behavior has a reason behind it, and your job is to find out why the sponsor is acting the way she is: • Is she just afraid of failure? Look at the guidance we offer for working with a sponsor who wants to be the project manager. • Does she not know better? See the sections on inexperienced and untrained sponsors, as well as the "Too Cool for School: Making Sponsorship Training Work" section in Chapter 7. • What if she doesn't believe in the project? See the section on the uninterested sponsor. Once you know that, you can better figure out what to do. If none of the above apply, you will have to do some additional work to validate the real reasons for her behavior. In the end, you may be left with a sponsor who actually wants to stop the project. What if this is the case? For everyone's benefit, this must be escalated to the highest level and a steering committee (project board) decision made about how the project will move forward (e.g., with a new sponsor or revised scope). Or perhaps it will be terminated after all. The PMO may be able to act as a third party to help mediate the sponsor–project manager relationship.

CASE NOTES: 1

I knew a head of development who decided that the only solution to the company's problems was to change its approach to software development and go Agile, adopting Scrum. The thing was, he *hated* Agile methods.

When discussing another department's progress in this area, he variously accused them of not doing Agile, and then later used them as an example of why adopting Agile doesn't work.

We never really understood the reason he took this approach, contrary to his own beliefs—perhaps it was because "Agile" was a hot topic? But the result was that he may have made the decision to go "Agile" but he didn't support the transition in any way at all.

CASE NOTES: 2

I knew a project sponsor who would blue-rinse[4] project reports such that projects would move from "red" to "amber" or "amber" to "green," thus making it seem as if a project was going better than it was and supplying falsified feedback from key stakeholders.

This had a very negative impact on the project managers he worked with, because it was impossible to escalate deviations from the project plan correctly and to obtain the right sponsorship decisions at the senior management level. They also felt complicit in lying to the organization. All of this combined meant that they were unable to manage their projects effectively. The sponsor and his team of project managers developed a bad reputation, and the organization challenged the project managers constantly; they were not believed when they were presenting accurate information.

The situation created a culture of fear and doubt, and we lost lots of good project managers as a result. The sponsor ended up being removed from this influential role and left the business.

CASE NOTES: 3

I worked on a project where I honestly thought that the project sponsor was attempting to sabotage the project. He was so difficult to work with and handled things so awkwardly every step of the way—through a lack of decision-making, micromanaging, constant worrying about every small part of the project, and not letting me, the project manager, do my job. It turned out that his job was on the line if the project was deemed a failure, and he was just scared it wouldn't be a success.

CASE NOTES: 4

One of the worst sponsors I've worked with directly caused a large project to fail. This was due to his manipulation of the role and the power that he perceived to be his as the sponsor; his behavior made it clear that he was not interested in the project or the expected benefits from it but instead thought only about the power and influence that being the sponsor would bring to him personally.

This sponsor ended up being fired. And sadly, he was actually a pretty good line manager, which was the reason his manager chose him to sponsor the project. Lesson was that a good functional manager does not necessarily a great sponsor make.

WHEN ALL ELSE FAILS

Sometimes, rarely—hopefully very, very rarely—you will manage a project with a sponsor who will just not work with you. What then?

First, make sure you have done all that you can to try to resolve the differences and work collaboratively. Have you

- Had general conversations about the project and talked about your hopes and dreams for it?
- Discussed roles and responsibilities?
- Reviewed project management plans and gained the sponsor's agreement?

- Developed a communication plan based on the sponsor's preferences?
- Kept all agreed-upon commitments from the plans?
- Been the trusted source of information for the sponsor?
- Used your influencing skills appropriately?
- Kept the sponsor informed of the project's needs?
- Emphasized that you have the same interest in project success?
- Given her feedback on specific things she has done that are impeding the project, and how they are affecting the project?
- Escalated specific issues, as appropriate, within your organization?

Still no luck? Unfortunately, this can and does happen. The first thing you have to remember is that right, wrong, or indifferent, the project sponsor is the ultimate authority for this project (unless, of course, you can get her kicked off or pushed out). This leaves you two options: accept the challenge or move on.

ACCEPT THE CHALLENGE

You're willing to accept that you have the sponsor you have, but you know that her actions are creating risks for the project. Document these risks as you would any other. You may also want to create a decision log, action log, journal, or other material to CYA.[5] This is not only a good contingency plan for you, but also provides valuable information about the project for the project team and stakeholders.

These logs may serve to help influence the sponsor, too. Let's say you have just logged the 101st decision change, and that day the sponsor asks you "Why is the project implementation date pushed back again?" Your log contains empirical evidence of the impact her actions are having on the project.

Be careful about how and with whom you share these logs. Publicly embarrassing your sponsor will not help your situation at all. Use the information within only if it can have a real impact on the project itself. It's about the project, not the person.

MOVE ON

At some point, you will decide it's time to move on. If you can get an internal transfer to a project with a different project sponsor, that's great. But it is more likely that you will need to spruce up your résumé or CV. Focus on the opportunities ahead and the benefits to your career, not the bad job experience you're trying to leave behind. This mindset will make you more marketable, help you avoid the sticky situation of discussing the unpleasantness in your current position during interviews, and make the "suck it up" days easier to get through as you look for a new job.

Take care when considering job offers. Do your homework, get to know the people you'd be working with, and try to get some informal references on them. And remember, the devil you know . . .

THE NOW AND WOW FACTOR

Here's a phenomenon that is guaranteed to happen to you at some time or another. You are working hard to manage a project, head down and spirits high, when your sponsor gets the hots for some new "now and wow"—some new method or initiative that she thinks will bring big benefits to the project. How do you handle this when it happens?

Let's look at an example involving one of the current "now and wows"—Agile software development methods. Your sponsor has just told you that she keeps hearing about this thing called "Agile," and she wants you to use it on your project. Now what?

The fact is, project sponsors often notice keywords and phrases and become excited, even if they have very little information about them.

Maybe your sponsor read an article about Agile online. What she may not realize is that the subject matter expert who wrote the article spent months or years learning and refining the tool and the method. So she is looking to you to replicate the success she read about.

Don't panic. We will guide you through the process of investigating the "now and wow," reporting on it, and influencing your sponsor toward the best solution for the situation. There are three basic steps:

1. Find out what your sponsor knows about the "now and wow." You can do this in your initial conversation on the topic, as below.

2. Use the information she provides and do your own research to analyze feasibility and develop a high-level plan.

3. Get her to agree to follow up on what you discover, without actually committing to do what she asked.

Your initial conversation with your sponsor might go something like this:

Sponsor: I want this project to be Agile. Can you do it?

PM: I probably can, but let me spend a little time figuring out what that would look like on this project. Let's start with a common understanding.

What do you mean by *Agile*? I would like to read the same books or article you have to make sure we are on the same page.

Sponsor: Oh, I'm not sure. CIO Robinson was bragging about how well it worked for her [competing] organization on their last project.

PM: Well, I see their PMO manager regularly at our local PMI meetings. I'll give him a call and see if he can do lunch so I can learn more about their processes and success. In the meantime, I will do a bit more investigation. Can we get together next week to discuss next steps?

Next, you need more information on what it really means to "do Agile." Many people believe that Agile projects do not require project managers or documentation. Your job is to sort through the information so that you can explain to your sponsor how the method would affect the project and provide a recommendation for moving forward.

Do you know a lot about Agile? If so, this will be a breeze. If not, familiarize yourself with the ins and outs. Talk to your peers and team members about Agile. Do they have experience with it? Network with experienced people in your industry. Look online for relevant articles, education opportunities, and consultants who can provide assistance.

Once you've educated yourself, you will be able to make a recommendation. Your recommendation will be the method you believe will maximize the project's potential for success and bring the greatest value to the business. Convincing your sponsor may take some work and salesmanship if your recommendation is different from what she initially wanted. Be candid yet sensitive to and understanding of her concerns.

There will be many "now and wow" tools, processes, and technology that could capture the interest of your sponsor. In any case, the following points are good general guidance when evaluating whether a hot new tool is right for your project:

- Listen to your sponsor to understand her request and expectations, and ask questions.

- Talk with your team and peers to learn about in-house experience.

- Network with others in your industry to learn about their experience.

- Look for resources that can provide professional assistance.

- Document what you have learned about the effects the tool or process will have on the project, including the constraints and risks.

- Present your recommendation to move forward to the sponsor.

- Have an open discussion to address concerns.

- Remember, the sponsor has the final word.

NOTES

1 The project management office, or PMO, in a business or professional enterprise is the department or group that defines and maintains the standards of process, generally related to project management, within the organization. The PMO strives to standardize and introduce economies of repetition in the execution of projects. See also Peter Taylor, *Leading Successful PMOs: How to Build the Best Project Management Office for Your Business* (Farnham, Surrey, UK: Gower, 2011).
2 *Project life cycle* refers to the commonly recognized stages of a project. You will find references to this throughout the *PMBOK® Guide*.
3 Adapted from Taylor, *The Lazy Project Manager*.
4 A blue rinse is a diluted hair dye used to reduce the yellowed (or translucent, showing scalp color) appearance of graying hair on older women. The ability to see blue decreases with age due to the development of cataracts, so an older woman may perceive her uncolored gray hair to have a yellow tinge, and the blue rinse brings the color back to an apparently normal color in her eyes.
5 The acronym *CYA* is used in the United States to mean "cover your ass." It is the process of documenting your and others' actions and the results so that when issues arise in the future, you can quickly and easily defend your own actions.

CHAPTER 4
Managing Your Project's Stakeholders

Stakeholders have the power to help or hurt your initiatives, so managing them is an essential part of project management. Your project sponsor is your number one stakeholder, but the strategies that are effective in working with your project sponsor will also work with other executive stakeholders—whether you have multiple sponsors, a project steering committee, or just very interested executives. We expand the discussion to additional stakeholders to better prepare the project manager for communicating across the organization to encourage project advancement and reduce risks and barriers.

Stakeholder management activities support an organization in achieving its strategic objectives. They include interpreting and influencing both the external and internal environments and building positive relationships with stakeholders through the appropriate management of their expectations and agreed-upon objectives.

STAKEHOLDER IDENTIFICATION

Stakeholders are interested parties either internal or external to the organization or project. Identification of stakeholders begins with the project sponsor, business owner, and project team. From there you broaden the net, asking each stakeholder "Who else has an interest in or is impacted by this project?" Review past project archives and lessons learned to see if you can identify other key stakeholders. Finally, take a look at the organization chart. Are there any units that could be impacted that are missing from your list, such as help desk support or training department? Missing stakeholder requirements is a common cause of failed projects. You will want to start with an exhaustive list. (The influence map discussed below will help make sense of which stakeholders will require the most work.)

STAKEHOLDER ANALYSIS

Stakeholder analysis is the process of recognizing and acknowledging each stakeholder's needs, concerns, wants, authority, common relationships, and interfaces. This information is used to create the *stakeholder matrix*. This matrix positions stakeholders according to their level of influence, or the ways in which they will affect or enhance the business or its projects through stakeholder engagement and in communicating information. An example is shown in Figure 4-1.

CHAPTER 4 • Managing Your Project's Stakeholders • 105

Stakeholder	Stake in the Project	Potential Impact on Project	What Does the Project Expect the Stakeholder to Provide?	Stakeholder Risks	Stakeholder Management Strategy	Managed by?
Name, Sponsor	Executive sponsor, approving scope, resources, and schedule for project	High	Resources adequate to complete project, guidance on priority, and resolution of any issues the team cannot resolve	Funding constraints and other IT needs may result in resource impacts	o Input to charter development o Monthly one-on-one status meetings o Monthly progress reports o Immediate heads-up notification of emerging issues that may affect scope, resources, or budget o One-on-one discussion for change control for scope, schedule, or budget	Project manager
Name, CIO	Oversight of organization IT and head of the portfolio committee	Medium	Resources	o Competing portfolio priorities o Budget reductions	o Invitation to Steering Committee meetings o Monthly progress reports o Completed charter for reference (includes change acceptance notices) o Investment plan for approval o Weekly combined report	Project manager

FIGURE 4-1: Stakeholder Matrix

Think of the stakeholder matrix as your very own database of relevant stakeholder information. You will not be able to capture full information upon first making an entry. As you learn more about the stakeholder and the project, additional information will become available for analysis. The stakeholder matrix should continue to grow throughout the project as you and the project team gain information. Update the matrix as you learn more about your stakeholders and the strategies and tools that work best for meeting their needs—as well as gaining their trust and cooperation. At the same time, update any project plans that can be improved, given what you know now. Plans were not meant to be set in stone but rather to be improved upon as additional information becomes available.

We have already stated that stakeholders have the power to help or hurt your initiatives, so managing them is an essential part of the project. We therefore suggest following these steps to develop your stakeholder analysis:

- Meet with the project sponsor and any other key stakeholders early on in the project and ask them "Who has a stake in this project, what is their interest, and what is their influence?"

- Begin documenting what you know about the stakeholders. Remember, project team members are stakeholders too.

- Review the organizational chart for the company and use your experience to identify additional potential stakeholders (e.g., network administrator, help desk support, accounting staff).

- Once your initial list is completed, send out an email introducing yourself and the project with an indication that they have been identified as stakeholders. Give them an opportunity to state their interests and communication preferences related to the project as well as provide information on additional stakeholders who may have been missed.

- Ask project team members and other key stakeholders to review the stakeholder matrix with you to provide additional information.

- Continually update the stakeholder matrix as you gain information throughout the life of the project. You may uncover a hidden key to the success of implementation while in the stabilization phase of product development. Record it, use it.

- Use the information in all planning activities. Use the information again in reviewing plans or conducting lessons learned to determine whether adjustments are needed.

Information is the key to success. Use the stakeholder matrix to structure your information gathering, record the information you learn, and pinpoint actions that will result in the greatest chances of project success. (Turn this information into an influence map for even greater effectiveness.)

STAKEHOLDER ENGAGEMENT

Stakeholder engagement is different from stakeholder management, in that engagement is not intended to develop project or business requirements, come up with problems or solutions, or establish roles and responsibilities. The primary purpose of engagement is for executive-level stakeholders to get to know and understand each other's goals and interest in the project. In the engagement process, stakeholders discuss and agree on expectations of communication and, most important, a set of values and principles by which all stakeholders will abide.

In the engagement phase, stakeholders establish agreed-upon expectations for the manner in which communications between stakeholders will be managed: who receives communications, when, how, and to what level of detail. Specific protocols also may be set, including security and confidentiality classifications.

THE INFLUENCE MAP

As is clear, the central question for the project manager is not just "Who are your stakeholders?" Stakeholders' identity is just one dimension. The real questions should be: "Do you understand who has influence over your projects? Do you know the strength of these influences?" Be forewarned that determining influences is not just a simple matter of looking at the organization chart and seeing who sits at the top of the pile. Influence is far more subtle and complex than that.

One tool we suggest is an *influence map*, which is a visual model that lays out in a simple format the people who influence and make decisions about a project. The map helps the project manager understand how stakeholders (including the sponsor) relate to one another and the associated influence flows: who affects whom, or who *could* affect whom and to what extent.

You can think of influence maps as a natural extension of a typical stakeholder analysis. A project's success can depend heavily on identifying key stakeholders and then managing the complex relationships between them and others on your project, all for the greater good and the most positive outcome. This is what influence mapping is all about—discovering the real stakeholders (not just the obvious ones) and the influence relationships between them and you, your project, and the business that sponsors the project.

It's important to know that even the most senior and ostensibly powerful people rarely like to act alone; it is in fact a rare authority figure who behaves this way. Top executives and other people in authority rely a great deal on advisers (internal or external), their peers, lobbying groups, and outside pressures. These relationships can form a complex web that an influence map can help you sort out.

You will need to consider three key elements when you put an influence map together:

1. The importance of each stakeholder's overall influence
2. The relationships between the stakeholders
3. The amount of influence stakeholders have over others.

EXAMPLE OF AN INFLUENCE MAP

Let's say that you are now in charge of a project to deploy a new global standard for all expense management inside your organization. You know this is a huge change, and you want to make sure it's well supported within the company before you try to implement it. You particularly want to understand the influence of the project sponsor who is leading this change. The sponsor is the chief financial officer (CFO), Roger Tuck, and he expects the project to simplify the process of expense management—submissions, analysis and validation, payment, and auditing.

On initial consideration, the most obvious stakeholders are as follows:

- CEO: Nigel Layseigh
- CFO: Roger Tuck

- VP of Sales: Lucy Trafford
- VP of Professional Services: Sonia Jay
- Director of Human Resources: Wilbur Collins

The next step is to think about whether there are other stakeholders, and who holds influence over whom. After further investigation, this is what you discover:

- The human resources (HR) team is barely involved in this project. In fact, Roger Tuck just told them about it. They have not been part of the project team selection process.
- Nigel Layseigh has delegated almost complete authority for this initiative to Roger Tuck and sees it as simply a finance project.
- The steering committee includes Lucy Trafford and Sonia Jay and is chaired by Roger Tuck.
- Also on the committee is Simon Duvard, an external independent consultant who advised Roger during the selection process for the expense application.
- Lucy Trafford and Sonia Jay have a history of conflict based on the tension between the sales organization, which is focused on dollar volume of sales in the short term, and the services/project organization, which has to deliver what the sales team has sold and focuses on the longer term.
- Lucy Trafford is very concerned about the new system. She does not want her sales team distracted by demands from the system; she just wants their expenses paid fast so that they can get on with their job. Sales has some of the highest expenses.

- Roger Tuck is concerned about the level of expenses in the sales department and wants control to be strengthened in this area; it is a key project objective.

- Nigel Layseigh is the former head of sales.

- Sonia Jay is worried the new system won't allow her consultants to record their expenses in a way that will allow them to easily re-charge their customers.

- The CEO, CFO, and VPs all have admin staff who process their own expenses for them.

The resulting influence map looks something like the one in Figure 4-2.[1]

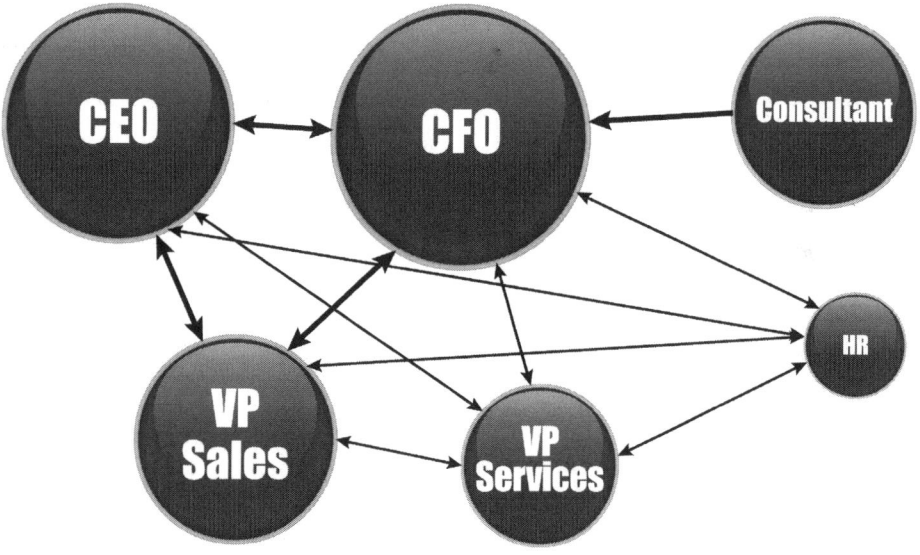

FIGURE 4-2: Example Influence Map

Circle = overall influence; line direction = effect of influence; line width = strength of influence.

This example influence map clearly shows that the CFO holds a lot of influence and power, and as the project manager, you might well be happy with this situation and consider Roger a "good" sponsor to have.

But the influence of the VP of sales on the CEO (remember, they're ex-colleagues with a shared sales background and focus), and to a lesser degree the influence of the VP of professional services on the CEO, will come into play at some point. The minimal involvement of HR means that the user community is individually represented by the VPs.

The high involvement during pre-selection and ongoing influence of the consultant on the CFO may well come into play at some point during the project and needs to be taken into account.

Before you considered the stakeholder influences, you might have assumed that the CEO and CFO had the most influence on organizationwide change. But the influence map shows you that this is probably not the case in this situation. The VP of sales is indeed a very important stakeholder, as indicated by the size of the circle and line widths indicating influence with the CEO and CFO.

Influence is not static. It changes over time, just like the circumstances surrounding each project or decision. If you create influence maps at regular intervals, you'll chart these differences and gain a much greater appreciation for the way decisions are made. This will help you to smooth the decision-making process and be a more effective project manager.

CREATING AN INFLUENCE MAP

Follow these eight steps to complete an influence map analysis for your project.

1. Prepare a stakeholder matrix to help you identify, prioritize, and understand all of your key stakeholders.

2. For all stakeholders, find out the following:
   - Whom do they influence, and who influences them?
   - How strong is that influence?
   - What is the history of each relationship, and how does this impact the stakeholders' influence on each other?
   - What role does hierarchy play in the influence relationships?

3. Map the importance of each stakeholder's influence:
   - Denote stakeholders with the most influence with larger circles.
   - Place the most influential stakeholders at the top of the page, and put less influential people lower on the page.

4. Map the direction of influences by drawing arrows to link the stakeholders. These may be one-way or two-way, depending on whether influence flows in both directions.

5. Map the strength of influence; use thicker lines to indicate stronger influence.

6. Study the map and identify the stakeholders with the most overall influence. Form a stakeholder management plan that will allow you to communicate with, and hopefully influence, these important influencers.

7. Remap these influence relationships on a regular basis to help you keep up with the dynamics of decision-making on the project.

8. Take some time to fully understand your project sponsor's place in the influence map. This will allow you to
   - Understand his strengths and weaknesses

- See who is most likely to influence him during the project
- Make informed and considered decisions about where to focus your own time on the project, based in part on your project sponsor's relationships and strength of influence.

We have seen many cases in which the wrong person was named sponsor, meaning that the title was given to somebody who did not have the appropriate level of interest or authority. This leads to many of the problems detailed in Chapter 3. An influence map will help you determine where to focus your communications to best get the support you need for your project—where to focus your energies in those situations where your sponsor is not the person with the greatest influence.

NOTES

1   A number of software tools can be used to build an influence map, but it is not difficult to put one together by hand that shows the key influencers.

When you reach the top, keep climbing.

—Proverb

PART II
For the Sponsor

CHAPTER 5
Sponsoring Your First Project

One day you will be invited to sponsor a project. In this chapter, we discuss how this can happen and what you can do to make the transition. We have already identified the types of challenging sponsors and provided actual stories as case notes. These stories highlight the important role played by the project sponsor.

If you are already a sponsor, this chapter is meant to function as a reality check for you—how are you doing in the role?

STORIES FROM THE STRATEGIES FOR SPONSORS SURVEY

We've given many negative examples in the previous chapters, but we must acknowledge that there are good project sponsors out there—maybe even folks that you, as a new or would-be project sponsor, can look up to and try to emulate. Here is an example of a great sponsor who worked in harmony with his project manager for the greater success of the project and business.

First, some background details. The project was to develop and implement a property management system for the retail division of a global property company. Here is the story as one contributor told it:

The initial project plan was at a high level, and the chief information officer (CIO) had agreed to it. I was already working within the company in a senior project manager role on a casual basis when the CIO asked if I'd manage this new project. The division that needed the solution had been waiting for a system for some time—at least two years—so there was a great deal of skepticism as the project commenced.

I briefly met with the sponsor, T.D., to discuss the current situation for his teams. Our discussion gave me a broad sense of the team structure for some 50 staffers, the various departments that would need to use the system, and the issues and business demands they faced. We also talked in some detail about what features would be useful, necessary, and ideal—"dreamed perfection."

We then talked about the requirements to run the project successfully. The key points we discussed were

- The team construct: who would represent each department and backup resources
- His availability, work commitments, and preferred method of working
- What I'd need from him as a sponsor:
    - Visibility
    - Decision-making
    - Arbitration
    - Championing the project at a senior level
    - Time to commit to meetings.

Before our first project meeting, we discussed my role as a PM. As a self-employed project manager, when I'm introducing myself to a new client, I begin by saying, "My job is to make myself redundant." More specifically, my job was to facilitate and complete the project—to ensure that the receiving organization is fully equipped to receive and use the deliverables (in the context of an IT project).

Our first project meeting consisted of meeting the team and establishing:

- **Who would be involved:** people who will make a small contribution
- **Who will contribute:** outside contractors or internal experts
- **Who will participate:** people or parts of the business who have to have their say.

After that meeting, I spoke with T.D. about the role he'd need to play. For example, when differences of opinion arose during team meetings, he would be the ultimate decision maker. He'd need to arbitrate and override opinions, passions, and agendas. Thankfully, he was more than able to do this.

During requirements development and build and test, we worked closely with a third party, a software company that was developing the solution for us. T.D. and I agreed on how we would manage email traffic:

- For all correspondence between me and the project team, he would be overtly copied in.
- For correspondence between me and the development team, he would be blind copied.
- Anything that needed his direct attention would be emailed to him directly.

He was brilliant! Rolled his sleeves up, got involved, gave insight and feedback, and made decisions promptly (and in writing). He was very accessible, and when he didn't have time to handle a matter in person, I emailed him to explain what I needed, and I could count on him to reply.

Project meetings were scheduled for an hour or two each Thursday morning. The project lasted 14 months, and he missed just five meetings, all while he was away on vacation. I couldn't have asked for more commitment from a business sponsor.

> His participation in meetings enabled me to facilitate a lively team with plenty of opinions, strong divergence in ideas and preferred solutions, and determination to have the system function just as they wanted it. The humor and commitment of the team members were undoubtedly a direct result of his visible commitment and personality.
>
> During the implementation of the system, T.D. became actively involved in testing; he participated in training and data entry and was instrumental in pushing for commitment and participation from the wider receiving audience. To encourage cooperation from people who were less committed, I contacted them initially and then reminded them of what we needed them to do. T.D. was visibly copied on those emails. I requested his intercession if there was continued resistance. Sometimes I composed the emails and then forwarded them to him, requesting that he be the "visible sender" in hopes that his formal authority would garner commitment.
>
> T.D. was forthright and very intense in his work and his determination. These qualities made us very compatible in working together, and despite the usual project challenges, he was a delight to work with. Undoubtedly, our similar work ethics, values, and commitment to success were contributory factors in the success of this project. In reflecting on my role as PM, he said, "She was a pain—and we couldn't have done the project without her." I consider that a success!

So that is how it is done. Easy, right? Well, no, but we can all see the benefit of working with such a project sponsor. Plenty of examples of those benefits can be found in the stories we received. Here are two more:

> We were designing a web-based order entry system for a customer support team. There had been a prototype, but we were not happy with it. Our sponsor was enthusiastic and stepped in to arrange a demo from a previous

employer of their web order system. The team came up with some great ideas based on the demo and felt so good about the sponsor playing such an active role in the design process that they worked hard to deliver the system.

Our sponsor was not prescriptive; she told us what the problems were as she saw them and then stepped away to let the project team figure out the best approach.

***

Our client was a state government entity on a fixed-price contract project. The lead sponsor on the project was a director-level person from the state team. He was very knowledgeable about the policies and procedures and had a great practical vision for what could be implemented. He used to spend hours and hours with project managers, business analysts, and even developers at times to explain the nuances of design and policy. He was one of the key success factors on the project. I was fortunate enough to work with such a sponsor; he really set the bar against which I evaluate other sponsors.

These stories just underscore what everyone believes: a good sponsor can significantly raise the likelihood of project success.

THE ACCIDENTAL PROJECT SPONSOR

We have all heard of the accidental project manager. This is the typical way in which any, shall we say, mature current project manager came to the role. Accidental project managers, just in case this is a term that is new to you, were people assigned to projects just because they were available, not because they had received any training in project management or indeed had any experience at all in project management. Some were successful, but many were blamed for project failures and problems despite the complete lack of support, guidance, and preparation that they received from their organizations. (Happily, things have very much improved for project managers in recent years.)

Now apply this concept to project sponsorship. Does it sound familiar?

You have reached a high level in your organization thanks to successes in sales, in manufacturing, in accountancy, in purchasing, in marketing, in operations, in leadership, or in strategic direction—in balancing the books and making the company successful. One day you are told that you will be a project sponsor, but you will not receive any training, support, guidance, or help. You have no experience to fall back on and perhaps no peers to even discuss your new job with. Congratulations! You are now an accidental project sponsor. You have taken the first step in educating yourself by reading this book.

TRANSITIONING FROM PROJECT MANAGER TO SPONSOR

What if you are a project manager who has just been tapped to serve as a sponsor? Just as it is not easy to stop being a technical consultant, a developer, or a hands-on team contributor and become a project manager, so too is it challenging for project managers to stop managing the project and assume a sponsorship role.

Look again at the list of a sponsor's typical responsibilities (shown again in Figure 5-1) and think about those where you will need to develop new skills, knowledge, or approaches. However, as with the previous sponsor responsibility assessment tool, why not take this a step further? Give the checklist to your colleagues or even a project manager and let them assess you. Collate the results and you will have real data to work on. The previous assessment had you evaluate how well your sponsor was meeting the sponsor responsibilities. Look at whether the responsibility will be an area of strength or weakness as you transition to this new role. Think about and note actions you can take to improve your strength relative to the responsibility.

Sponsor Responsibility	Areas to Improve
1. Provides direction and guidance for strategies and initiatives	
2. Works with the project manager to develop the project charter	
3. Identifies and quantifies business benefits to be achieved by successful implementation of the project	
4. Makes go/no-go decisions	
5. Evaluates the project's success upon completion	
6. Negotiates funding for the project	
7. Actively participates in the initial project planning	
8. Reviews and approves changes to plans, priorities, deliverables, schedule, and more	
9. Identifies project steering committee members	
10. Gains agreement among stakeholders when differences of opinion occur	
11. Chairs the project steering committee	
12. Assists the project when required (especially in an out-of-control situation) by exerting organizational authority and the ability to influence	
13. Helps resolve interproject boundary issues	

Sponsor Responsibility	Areas to Improve
14. Supports the project manager in conflict resolution	
15. Advises the project manager of protocols, political issues, and potential sensitivities	
16. Makes the project visible within the organization	
17. Encourages stakeholder involvement and builds and maintains their ongoing commitment through effective communication strategies	

FIGURE 5-1: Sponsor Responsibility Improvement Needs Assessment

Eugene Bounds, senior vice president at Booz Allen Hamilton and 2010 PMI board chairman, summed up the differences as a matter of vision, tactical or strategic:

> The project manager looks at the project tactically. He or she looks more in the weeds of the project or the details to try to get it done. The executive sponsor tends to look at it as a strategic event. . . . He or she will look at the project on how it aligns with the goals of the organization.[1]

The project manager's and project sponsor's duties are obviously different and clearly delineated, and both parties need to think within their own boxes, yet they are partners and must work as one for the success of the project.

TAKING SPONSORSHIP SERIOUSLY

The Standish Group reminds us that the sponsor is "the owner of the project."[2] As the owner of the project, the full weight and responsibilities of the success or failure of the project fall squarely on your shoulders. For better or worse, you own the outcome and have no right to abdicate your executive responsibility.

The sole responsibility for a successful outcome rests on the shoulders of the executive sponsor. The sponsor may not be an executive of the organization, but she is the chief executive of the project. The word *executive* symbolizes a higher level of responsibility. It is more powerful than just *sponsor*.[3]

Think of your relationship with the project manager as a collaboration where you have equal interest in the success of the project and are each other's primary support in achieving the goal. You are partners in an "amazing race"[4] and can win the game only if you trust and respect each other and when you leverage each other's strengths and weaknesses.

Figure 5-2 shows one view of how a project sponsor fits into the project organization. His particular responsibility is to bring value to the business.

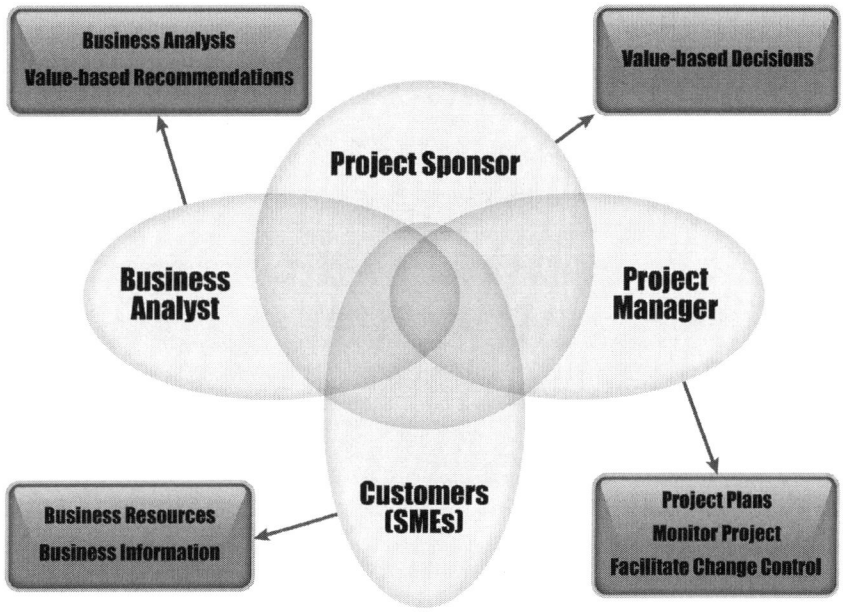

FIGURE 5-2: Project Responsibilities

SPONSORSHIP IS REAL WORK

When it comes to financial accountability, it seems—at least anecdotally—that projects often go over budget, deliver late, and deliver less than was expected . . . and there are absolutely no consequences. No one appears to be accountable and no one gets removed.

Now, if something goes wrong in the "real" side of the business—sales down, profits falling, share price dropping—then it seems like something will be done and someone will be held accountable. Maybe this is because this is seen as "real" business and "real" work and as such has to be taken seriously.

Project sponsorship needs the same strength of focus and importance of status. The success or failure of a project is a direct reflection on the sponsor (or the project manager's ability to influence the sponsor) as the keeper of the organizational vision and checkbook.

Eileen Roden, head of project management learning at QA Ltd, one of the United Kingdom's longest-established project management training companies, told us, "Sponsorship is not an extra . . . *it is* the day job." Sponsors need to think this way in order to do a good job for the business they represent and the projects that they sponsor.

ASKING FOR GUIDANCE

Consider this: if your job were on the line based on the results of the project you are sponsoring, how much more carefully would you consider accepting the role in the first place? How much more open would you be to receiving support and guidance in performing your sponsorship duties? If the stakes are high, all of us spend a lot more time considering the potential risks and the impact of failure.

Many of us have a lot of years of experience behind us (perhaps more behind us than in front of us these days), but that doesn't keep us from seeking professional advice in a lot of situations. We seek

- Legal advice when faced with a legal problem
- Financial advice when considering mortgage plans, pension plans, or investment decisions
- Medical advice when feeling unwell or concerned about our health.

We don't want to ignore a minor ailment and let it develop into something potentially life threatening. We don't want to risk investing all of our money in a bad scheme that will leave us impoverished. And we don't want to get involved in a legal dispute, representing ourselves badly and leaving ourselves exposed to negative consequences. We ask others for guidance in these cases because we want to make the best decisions possible, and we know that by asking, listening, and then acting, we will be better off. And there is no stigma attached to seeking such advice.

The same is true regarding your role as a sponsor: you should not be afraid to seek advice on sponsorship matters. Your project manager is your local project expert. Rely on his expertise and recommendations to keep your project on track. But unless there are real consequences to sponsors for project failure—unless they have skin in the game, so to speak—some sponsors will not be motivated to ask for help. This apathy can damage the reputation and track record of the sponsor as someone who can get things done.

When we've asked participants at presentations whether they strive to be mediocre in their jobs, no one raises their hand. But when we ask, "Who strives to excel at their job?" all hands are raised. Perhaps your own desire for excellence will drive you to seek guidance when you need it.

NOTES

1. Jim Johnson, "The Good Sponsor," *Software Magazine* (November 2012), http://www.softwaremag.com/content/ContentCT.asp?P=3422.
2. The Standish Group, *Chaos Manifesto 2012: The Year of the Executive Sponsor* (Boston: The Standish Group, 2012), 3.
3. Ibid.
4. *The Amazing Race* is a US game show on which pairs of contestants participate in a worldwide scavenger hunt for a prize of $1 million.

CHAPTER 6
Sponsor Responsibilities and Best Practices

In this chapter, we detail many of the sponsor responsibilities listed in the Sponsor's Responsibilities Evaluation Tool (Figure 2-2) and share some related best practices, ones that project managers wish their sponsors understood. These best practices are based on decades of experience in project management and have been passed down project manager to project manager through organizations such as the Project Management Institute and the Association for Project Management. We believe in these best practices and have seen the benefits that they bring to our projects (or perhaps the chaos that has ensued when they are not followed).[1]

If you are a project manager, you will be familiar with the processes and concepts described here. You may find this section to be a good reference for communicating with your sponsor about his role. If you are a sponsor, this section can help you understand the role you've been given.

PROVIDING DIRECTION AND GUIDANCE STRATEGIES AND INITIATIVES

As the project owner, the sponsor understands how the project will help the organization achieve its goals. The sponsor must be able to explain how the project fits into the organization's overall strategic plan. This includes providing information on how the project aligns with the objectives, goals, mission, and vision of the organization. This may also include discussion of downstream strategies that the project helps feed. Providing this context to the project team and stakeholders will

- Help ensure activities and recommendations related to the project are in alignment with the strategic direction
- Aid project staff in helping promote the project
- Motivate project staff with knowledge of how their daily work contributes to the organization
- Set the stage for future related strategies
- Provide context for championing the project to stakeholders
- Validate the value of the project within the context of the organization's strategic plan.

Consider the importance of strategic alignment when developing the project charter, reviewing and providing feedback on project plans, and making decisions on scope changes or other corrective actions. Focusing project efforts around the organization's strategic goals will ensure that the project best meets them.

WORKING WITH THE PROJECT MANAGER TO DEVELOP THE PROJECT CHARTER

As the project's owner, the sponsor has the ultimate responsibility and authority over the project. The charter is the sponsor's formal agreement to the project. Most of the time, the project manager drafts the project charter based on her understanding of the project. The sponsor must actively work with the project manager to ensure that both of them have mutual understanding of the project and will then sign the final charter as the formal artifact of project approval. This document should contain

- A statement of the business problem or opportunity to be addressed
- How the project supports the organization's overarching strategies and objectives
- Quantified business benefits to be achieved
- The project governance structure, with roles and responsibilities
- Schedule, budget, and scope constraints
- High-level risks
- The name of the project manager
- Approval to begin the project.

IDENTIFYING AND QUANTIFYING BUSINESS BENEFITS TO BE ACHIEVED

Although anticipated business benefits are a component of the aforementioned charter (as well as the business case that preceded it), they warrant further discussion. Identifying and quantifying business benefits are the greatest tools you have to keep the project focused and avoid scope creep. All project decisions can be weighed against these metrics if they have been documented.

Early in the project life cycle, you should determine and document the expected outcomes of the project. Ideally, this is done when a business case is being developed and submitted. This step defines "project success" and is critical to the project charter. Here are some questions to consider:

- What is the problem or opportunity that the project is addressing?
- What will have changed for the business after successful implementation?
- How will you know it has changed?

Consider the following scenario. You are sponsoring a project to develop and implement a new training registration system within your organization. The project was proposed to address concerns that it takes too much staff time to register students; as a result, staff have had to work extra hours and are falling behind in other duties. You recognize that decreasing needed staff time will create the largest return on investment to the organization. Your business analyst (or project manager) works with you to articulate the following project outcomes, documented in the project charter:

1. Reduce overall staff time required per student registration by 75 percent.
2. Time to complete inquiry of student participation should be not more than 10 minutes (from "opened" to "responded").

The project manager comes to you with a change request from marketing to provide an export of data from the system to be used for direct mailings. The cost of the change request is $25,000 and adds two weeks to the schedule. While the request is a good idea, it does not support the expected outcomes of this project. The request should be denied, using this justification as elaborated below.

Having the expected outcomes of the project clearly stated in the charter gives you the leverage you need to deny the request without appearing to be unhelpful. You may be thinking, "Why would I deny something that clearly will bring some benefit to the organization?" You should deny it because the change introduces new risks, reduces your project contingency, and increases the likelihood that the project will become "challenged." Remember, responsibility for this project is yours alone as the owner of the project; you are the only person who can overturn the project manager's recommendation. The sponsor has a duty to isolate the project from new risks, and the top three causes of "challenged" projects are poor requirements, lack of executive support, and scope changes.[2]

Alternatively, marketing could put in a new project request for the data export once your project is complete and implemented. Then you will likely have two successful projects instead of one challenged project.

MAKING GO/NO-GO DECISIONS

Projects take time to plan and deliver. Over the course of this time, you may find that the project you're working on will no longer provide the value to the business that was originally intended. Maybe this is because of changes in the project, or factors external to the project that have changed the impact the completed project will have on the organization. For example:

> Your organization has chartered a project for a new customer relationship management (CRM) system to be developed in-house. The project team spent three months planning the project, while the business analysis group elicited requirements. At that point, you had spent $50,000.

Eventually, the business analysts came back with the prioritized requirements, and the project team expended significant effort in estimating the work needed to meet the requirements. The refined estimates indicate that the project will take 50 percent longer and cost 50 percent more than provided in the early order-of-magnitude estimates. In the meantime, you hear of a competing organization that has implemented a cloud-based, software-as-a-service CRM solution with great success.

Should this project continue?

A project sponsor needs to be able to ask the hard questions, review the data, and make the decision that will bring the most value to his business. The natural instinct will be to continue the project, believing that cancellation really means failure. Some sponsors may be reluctant to cancel because doing so makes them feel as if they have wasted money. The truth is that money spent is money spent (sunk cost). Instead of focusing on the money lost, the sponsor needs to ask two questions:

- How much more money and time would it take to complete and implement the current CRM project, compared with the money and time it would take to stop the project and then recharter with a software-as-a-service solution?
- Which of these two options will bring the most value to the business?

In this example, the best approach is to issue a change request to add scope for a feasibility study to compare the two options. At the conclusion of the feasibility study, the sponsor should either replan or baseline the current development project or cancel the development project and start a new project for the software-as-a-service CRM implementation.

EVALUATING THE PROJECT'S SUCCESS UPON COMPLETION

Assessing completed projects may fall to the project management, portfolio management, or business analysis functions within the organization, at the direction of the project sponsor. Evaluating successful completion goes beyond asking if the team finished on time, within budget, and within the agreed-to scope. Think of the last project implemented more than six months ago in which you were involved. Has this project been reviewed to compare the actual results to the objectives identified in the business case or project charter? If it has, you are one of the lucky few who have the satisfaction of knowing you not only saw a project to completion, but that the project most likely met the expected outcomes as chartered.

Would you rather be the sponsor who brought a project in on time, on budget, and within scope, but did not meet objectives or the sponsor whose project brought value to the organization? The problem is that we do not often have a view into our past projects to know how we did. But we can find out by simply reviewing the project's actual benefits achieved once the project has been implemented for several months.

Organizations need to monitor completed projects over time to track their success in delivering value. Tracked data will help organizations make better project decisions in the future. For example, strong change management processes will continue to be supported if projects with good change management processes that allow for value-added changes in a controlled fashion tend to bring more value to the organization.

The benefits of this information would be immense if it were coupled with formal review of prior lessons learned (but that's another book).

NEGOTIATING FUNDING FOR THE PROJECT

The sponsor is the keeper of the funding for the project. Look back at Figure I-1 for a simplified illustration of how projects are typically funded and approved. The funding is entrusted to the project sponsor, who charters the work, selects the project manager, and authorizes the project to begin.

The entire process begins when a project is just an idea and the business case is developed. The sponsor's first responsibility is to decide which business cases will bring the business the most value and then campaign for organizational funding. The organization then provides the funding to the sponsor to manage. In some cases, the sponsor may fund the project out of his own approved budget, but the effect is the same: funding the project is within the sponsor's budget authority.

The diagram in Figure 6-3 suggests standards for how much variance a project estimate may have during different stages of the project effort. Predicting project cost is much like predicting the weather: Both are complex systems with many unknowns. Projects are often funded as if the final figure for the completed project will and should match the original estimate exactly. In reality, not enough information is known about any project to provide an estimate with any level of certainty until the requirements and design have been completed. This level of detail takes a considerable amount of time and money to determine, and an estimate based on this information should be completed as part of the project, or a project phase. Each phase estimate should be expressed in terms of a range based on the phase of the project, as outlined in the figure. The only 100-percent-accurate estimate is for work that is completed—the actual cost.

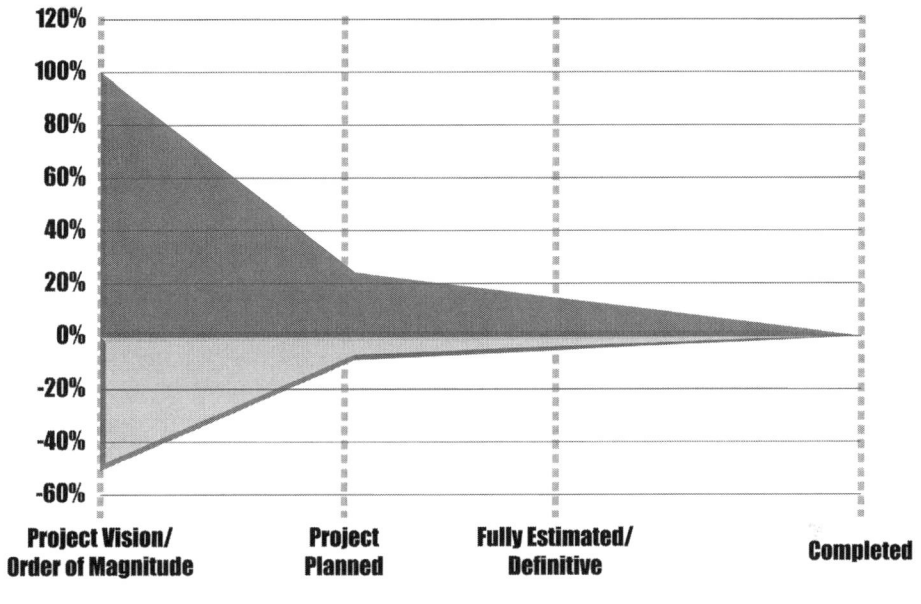

FIGURE 6-3: The Cone of Uncertainty

ACTIVELY PARTICIPATING IN INITIAL PROJECT PLANNING

The project manager is in charge of planning the project, but the sponsor has a role in setting and reviewing project plans. A project plan should meet the sponsor's expectations regarding communication, change requests, risk management, resources, schedule, budget, and procurement of all required project resources.

REVIEWING AND APPROVING CHANGES TO PLANS, PRIORITIES, DELIVERABLES, SCHEDULE, AND MORE

No matter what you do to prevent changes, they will inevitably hit your project. Accordingly, there needs to be a clear process for ensuring any changes made are acceptable. The project manager (or other person making the change request) should complete a change request form which is then reviewed by the project team to determine impact on scope, schedule, budget, and risk. The sponsor is the person who approves any changes. No work should be done unless a change request has been agreed to and identified impacts accepted.

A special note to sponsors: Project managers tell us that sponsors are often the worst violators of this rule. They often want to make changes to the project without going through the change control process. If you're a project manager, you may well need to impress the importance of the process upon your sponsor. If you're a sponsor, please stick to the process.

IDENTIFYING PROJECT STEERING COMMITTEE MEMBERS

A steering committee (sometimes called a *project board*) should be small, with around five members. The sponsor is the person responsible for identifying and selecting the appropriate people to sit on this committee.

Clear criteria need to be set out for selecting the right people. It should be a deliberate choice to invite person X or Y to sit on the committee. Also, check each prospective committee member's availability for meetings. We have seen people selected for committees who never attend the meetings because they are constantly traveling.

Once established, a clear role for the committee needs to be agreed on by committee members. This should include who makes what decisions as well as the kinds of information the project manager needs to prepare to support discussions and decisions. As discussed below, the project sponsor chairs the steering committee.

CHAIRING THE PROJECT STEERING COMMITTEE

This is a key role for the project sponsor. The committee will meet by agreement. These should be formal meetings, with an agenda and action points. Meetings should be well run and brief, and the key issues identified early. The sponsor can help make this happen by letting the project manager know ahead of time what must be accomplished in each meeting.

The sponsor should keep in mind that it is not just his role as chair that is under the microscope; the steering committee's actions also may be scrutinized by organization executives or external stakeholders, possibly including the media and public.

ASSISTING THE PROJECT WHEN REQUIRED

Sometimes a project goes out of control for whatever reason. The project sponsor needs to show real authority and leadership when this happens. First, clear parameters must be set for the project manager to inform the sponsor as soon as some part of the project goes out of control. (The sponsor and project manager have to agree on a definition of *out of control* beforehand.)

Once it is known that the project is out of control, the sponsor has to work to understand the issues that have arisen, and he and the project manager need to discuss and agree on corrective action. This may include rescoping the project, stopping the project, or ensuring there are more resources (including money) devoted to resolving the problems.

It goes without saying that the sponsor will need to devote additional time to the project and helping the project manager when project control is lost.

ASSISTING WITH THE RESOLUTION OF INTERPROJECT BOUNDARY ISSUES

Those in the project community tell us that interproject boundary issues come up often. Project managers tell us that they find these issues very difficult and time consuming to deal with.

Often, the sponsor needs to liaise with another sponsor or project manager to sort out real boundary management issues. It's important to note that the project manager cannot sort out this issue alone. The matter has to be escalated and dealt with by the sponsor.

SUPPORTING THE PROJECT MANAGER IN CONFLICT RESOLUTION

It is not uncommon for project managers to say that they sometimes feel quite alone in dealing with conflict. They admit to not having the knowledge or the training to sort out what are often really difficult situations. The sponsor needs to support the project manager when any conflicts or disputes arise. It is difficult to say exactly what that support should involve because each situation will be different.

After a conflict is resolved, the sponsor should use the lessons learned from the situation to train and coach the project manager.

MAKING THE PROJECT VISIBLE WITHIN THE ORGANIZATION

Another key role for the project sponsor is ensuring that the project is championed within the organization. The sponsor must be proactive in talking about any projects he is sponsoring. His public commitment to the project can make all the difference in the project team's and other stakeholders' perception of the importance of the project to the organization.

One project manager offers an idea for encouraging a sponsor to promote a project. The project manager developed a draft presentation (a few PowerPoint slides) about the project that he suggested the sponsor could present at four management meetings she was to attend. The sponsor liked the idea and presented the project talk to all four groups, helping to raise awareness and the visibility of the project.

ENCOURAGING STAKEHOLDER INVOLVEMENT AND BUILDING AND MAINTAINING ONGOING COMMITMENT

Beyond making the project visible within the organization, the sponsor needs to ensure that all of the project stakeholders are committed to the effort. By engaging with stakeholders in accordance with the overall project communications strategy, and by constantly giving out messages about the project, the sponsor demonstrates his ownership and ongoing commitment to the project.

Differences of opinion are inevitable, and the project sponsor's role comes to the forefront when they arise. The sponsor needs to work with the project manager and stakeholders to obtain agreement, especially when political issues come up.

Sometimes, stakeholders are senior people who will not engage too well with the project manager, or if they do, they will pull rank. The sponsor has to be aware of these attitudes and proactively work with the project manager to get agreement. Often, the sponsor's authority plays a role in conflict resolution.

But you cannot and will not please all of the people all of the time, and sometimes tough decisions have to be made. If time is short and a decision has to be made without securing agreement first, the project sponsor must show some leadership by making the decision that supports the project and the project manager. Always publicly show support of the project manager to retain trust in the relationship.

ADVISING THE PROJECT MANAGER ABOUT PROTOCOLS, POLITICAL ISSUES, AND POTENTIAL SENSITIVITIES

A sponsor is usually a senior person within the company, and with that seniority (we hope) comes awareness of the complex, sometimes covert political issues that arise within companies. There are also company protocols that need to be followed, and it is the sponsor's duty to inform the project manager about what is required. (We know that sometimes the project manager is the one doing the educating, but it does not matter who does it as long as it's done.)

The exchange of information between the sponsor and the project manager regarding protocol and political issues has a number of benefits, one of which is the education of both parties; another is that they can avoid potentially embarrassing situations.

NOTES

1   The Standish Group, *Chaos Manifesto 2012: The Year of the Executive Sponsor* (Boston: The Standish Group, 2012), 3.

An organization's ability to learn, and translate that learning into action rapidly, is the ultimate competitive advantage.

—Jack Welch

PART III
For the Organization

CHAPTER 7
Developing the Sponsor

We have explained in previous chapters what the role of the sponsor is and why the role is so important. We now need to move toward looking at what will help organizations develop great sponsors and set the company up for project success.

TOO COOL FOR SCHOOL: MAKING SPONSORSHIP TRAINING WORK

Let's take for granted that sponsors need some form of training for the role. But what sort of training do sponsors accept?

In one organization, there was an initiative to deliver sponsorship training. Human Resources (HR) and the project community identified a two-day course and scheduled it. Several members of the senior management team—from which sponsors were regularly chosen—were to attend so that they could learn about how to be a good project sponsor should they be selected to do so.

As word got out about the course, pressure came from the would-be students, through the HR representative, to reduce it to just one day. The training provider agreed to create a one-day course; after all, these were busy people and it was important to take that into account.

The week before the training, there came a second wave of pressure to reduce the duration of the course even more. "Real" work was demanding the executives' time and focus, and they really couldn't afford to be away from their desks for one full day.

The one-day course was further reduced to just half a day.

When the training day arrived, most of the management team "attended" the session, but the BlackBerry activity and the "slipping out for an important call" disruptions were so significant that the course was stopped partway through the morning, and the students escaped, no doubt with a sense of relief.

It must be acknowledged that in some companies, the classroom approach is not going to be effective. In other companies, it will work really well. It is important to look at your audience and consider the best approach for them in terms of their development, the time available, and their motivation—you can do this through personal knowledge of them or through advice from your HR team, or even by talking to them directly. For some senior managers, training needs to be provided in a very nontraditional way. Courses, electronic learning, and books (even this one)[1] won't work for them. They are clearly "too cool for school"—so what is the right way? Coaching, preceded by a short analysis of development needs, would be a really positive approach.

In another case, a company decided on the coaching route for prospective sponsors. The organization's senior managers were not only too cool for school but, according to the company, too senior and too well-paid to take time off for training. It is important to stress, although the company took the coaching approach, this was not the normal style for such employee development, as the company culture (financial services) was far removed from this approach. The program management office (PMO) saw the value in coaching these senior people but called it "information-giving sessions."

A PMO staff member started the process by visiting each senior manager who would be impacted by key company projects. He explained the project management approach people would be using and the impact the approach and the projects would have on them as senior executive managers and key stakeholders:

- The projects had risks that would affect the senior managers' department and teams within it. (This was a financial services company, and the managers eventually began to appreciate how project management fit well with their professional risk management approach.)

- The projects would affect the availability of professional staff, who would be working to deliver key company change projects. The PMO staff member emphasized the need for the managers to engage with staff in the overall planning of projects, especially putting the project plans together.

As the various projects progressed, the program management office staffer visited the senior managers more often, and they started to appreciate new ways of working such as using change control processes. Previous to coaching, senior managers would demand changes to projects while ignoring the internal need for change requests. The result was that some projects inevitably went over budget and past the delivery date.

They received invitations to project update meetings. Some attended, some did not. Eventually, the role of project sponsor was talked about more openly and in more detail. Over a period of time (approximately 18 months), sponsors started to emerge and play their role very effectively. They recognized that *not* playing their role was not an option; it led to increased costs and late delivery. For this company, a very slow-paced coaching route paid off.

A two-tier approach might be appropriate, with two different focuses: one for "junior" executives, who might be eager to learn and would welcome an event-based training approach, and one for "senior" executives, who might have an "I have already made it, and I know what I need to know" attitude and can only be gently encouraged to see that gaining more appreciation of what sponsors do is necessary.

What should such training (or, with regard to the senior executives, subtle coaching) cover? Among other elements, the topics should include:

- Project overview
- The sponsor's relationship with the project manager
- Creating the project charter
- Project kickoff
- Roles and responsibilities
- What do sponsors need to approve?
- When do sponsors need to get involved?
- How to recognize a good project plan
- How to recognize a good scope statement
- Project risks and how to manage them
- Change management

- Keeping projects on track
- Milestone reviews and quality assurance
- Lessons learned/retrospectives.

When considering training, think about both the needs of the project sponsor(s) and their preferred learning styles. For training to work, it has to be tailored to an individual's time, availability, priority of need, and preferred style of communication. Work with your project sponsors to develop an approach and plan that meets both your needs; utilize all other resources inside your organization, such as HR or a training team, that can help you make this happen.

FIFTY SECRETS TO BEING A GOOD PROJECT SPONSOR

You already know that this is not a lightweight or spare-time (as if busy C-level executives actually have any spare time!) type of role, but something that is meaty and demanding and critical to the organization. We once again visit The Standish Group's *CHAOS Manifesto 2012: The Year of the Executive Sponsor* for a list of 50 key skills, or "secrets," to being a good executive sponsor.[2]

THREE SECRETS

Each of these 50 skills will make a positive impact on the organization; we provide the full list later in this chapter. We considered the 50 skills and chose three to discuss in detail:

- Secret 3: Understand the project management process
- Secret 9: Reward outstanding effort

- Secret 42: Track progress against plan.

A brief description is given below of each of these "secrets" together with our thoughts on what the secret really means.

SECRET 3: UNDERSTAND THE PROJECT MANAGEMENT PROCESS

The 2012 CHAOS Survey asks a question: "How skilled are you at knowing and gaining understanding of your project management process?" Our experience shows that many project sponsors do not have basic knowledge of such processes.

Now, we do not expect every sponsor to understand every nuance, every process, or every template that needs completing, but we do see it as a key knowledge area for sponsors.

If the sponsor is to own the project and have the full weight and responsibility for the success or failure of the project on her shoulders, then she should understand the project management process. Some basic education (see "Too Cool for School") is needed to ensure that the sponsor can not only take responsibility but also promote the project in the organization.

Take the situation where the sponsor goes to a meeting and there is criticism of the project. "It's going too slowly!" says one person. But what this person does not know—and the sponsor does—is that the project management process expects testing to take place. You are in the middle of a large-scale test to ensure that the project is not only delivered on time but also works when it is delivered. The sponsor can use this to explain the overall process to others. The sponsor has been placed in this situation because she understands the project management process. Without this basic knowledge the sponsor will find the project difficult to promote and cannot take full responsibility for it.

SECRET 9: REWARD OUTSTANDING EFFORT

The sponsor is in a unique position to see what is and is not being done to deliver a project. We listened to the many stories that show project teams and project managers "going the extra mile" to ensure project delivery. The sponsor is the person who should recognize and reward outstanding effort.

We are not suggesting the reward should be financial (though it can be, if the sponsor feels it is appropriate). However, positive recognition can make a huge impact on project morale and progress. Over the years, we have seen different ways of rewarding outstanding effort both to encourage similar behavior in others and just to deliver that "Well done!" Some rewards that were popular included

- A trip to a local attraction for a project team that had just delivered a very tricky stage of a project successfully (e.g., the London Eye, Pike Place Market, Disneyland)

- An overnight trip to a local destination for the successful completion of a project (e.g., London to Paris, Los Angeles to Las Vegas)

- A photograph in the company magazine with a description of what the team had achieved

- A team meeting with the sponsor rather than the usual one-to-one with the project manager and the meeting followed by a pizza lunch

- The sponsor physically taking a cake to members of the project team and thanking them for their efforts.

Each of these had a really positive impact on project team members; however, each also had a positive organizational impact. In the case of the sponsor taking cakes around to each person, it was reported that the organization was buzzing and other sponsors were looking at what they could do to motivate and reward effort.

One final thought on this "secret." Many project managers told us that a "thank you" from their sponsors would be appreciated. Many do not receive one! Is this a lost opportunity?

SECRET 42: TRACK PROGRESS AGAINST THE PLAN

In *The Chaos Manifesto*, The Standish Group points out that 47 percent of executive sponsors found it difficult or very difficult to master the skill of understanding the project tracking system.[3]

There needs to be collaboration between the project sponsor and the project manager on the amount and type of information that the sponsor needs. The Standish Group concludes that this does not occur as frequently as it should. It suggests that sponsors can help themselves by taking the time to say, up front, how they want progress measured: "Executive sponsors need to tell the programme manager the requirements they need so they can effectively provide oversight."[4]

Without data on project progress, a project may well receive more investment when it should really be stopped or steered in a different direction.

Each of these secrets affects the organization in its own way:

- **Understanding the project management process.** Without this understanding (by the sponsor), a project could get bogged down with changes and amendments and fail to deliver or to meet its strategic objectives.

- **Rewarding outstanding effort.** All staff, including project staff, need to be well motivated and feel they are valued. A lack of reward could result in loss of key project staff, having a negative impact on the project and organization.

- **Tracking progress.** Often the organization requires data or information that the sponsor must provide on the project progress. However, as discussed, the information needs of the sponsor will be different from those of the project manager. If the sponsor does not have the right information, then bad decisions could be made that impact the whole organization.

A BALANCED SPONSORSHIP COMPETENCY FRAMEWORK

We also compared the 50 "secrets" to our thoughts on what makes for a "balanced" sponsor, as shown in Figure 7-1. Some of the case studies of project sponsorship that we explored in Chapter 3 demonstrate an unbalanced approach to sponsorship. That is, they describe a focus of effort and interest in just one area and show the negative effect of this disproportionate focus on the project manager and on the project. Conversely, the "balanced" project sponsor will consider and act in a way that brings an equal focus on a number of areas of sponsorship responsibility.

158 • STRATEGIES FOR PROJECT SPONSORSHIP

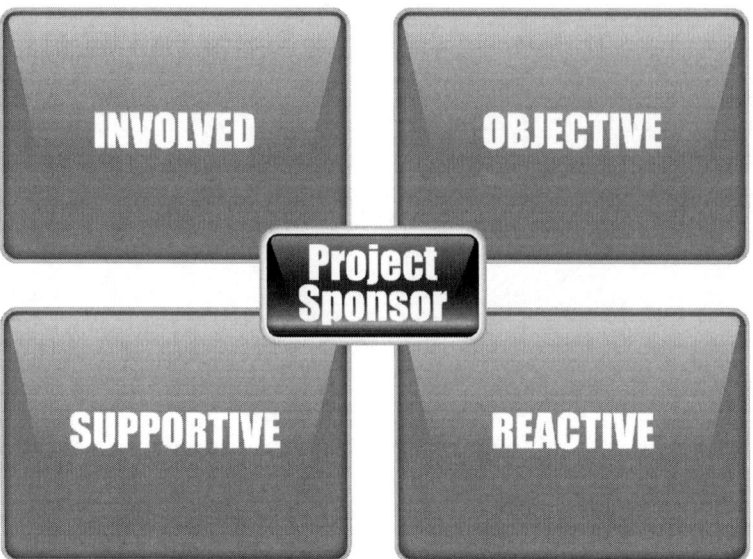

FIGURE 7-1: Balanced Sponsor Competency Framework

If we connect each of the four focus areas of balanced project sponsorship capability shown in the figure—being *involved* in the project, being *objective* about the project, being *supportive* of the project and project manager, and being *reactive* to project needs—to The Standish Group's 50 secrets, we arrive at these key secrets:

1. Involved:
    - Secret 1: Inspire
    - Secret 2: Know How the Solution Will Be Used
    - Secret 36: Have Commitment

2. Objective:
    - Secret 7: Understand Business Events
    - Secret 10: Provide Clarity of Purpose
    - Secret 17: Demand Objectivity and Transparency

3. Supportive:
   - Secret 3: Understand the Project Management Process
   - Secret 33: Celebrate Accomplishments
   - Secret 43: Create a Community

4. Reactive:
   - Secret 9: Reward Outstanding Effort
   - Secret 12: Obtain Decision Acceptance
   - Secret 16: Make Quick Decisions

For your reference, the complete list of 50 secrets from The Standish Group are presented in Appendix D. Please refer to the published report[5] for additional information on The Standish Group's findings and information.

Look at that list and then ask yourself why so many businesses believe, or act as if they believe, that an executive who has reached a certain position within the organization (perhaps C-level, at least senior level) will naturally have all of those skills in place and just waiting to be used in a sponsoring role?

Would you fill the role of chief financial officer inside your company with someone who has had no experience or training in business accounting and finance and who has not been appropriately certified, just because she is X years old, has Y years of working experience, and is pretty good at Z (where Z is anything but finance)?

C-level executives who want their strategy delivered through project-based activity need to understand and appreciate the link with effective sponsorship in delivering strategic success.

DEVELOPING YOUR ORGANIZATION'S SPONSORSHIP CAPABILITY

Those from the project community, particularly project managers, can have a significant role in influencing the organization's executive management to invest in developing sponsors.

WHAT PROJECT MANAGERS CAN DO

One duty project managers have as experts in best project management practices is to promote best practices within their organizations. This means speaking up and promoting best practices when the organization is not employing them. If you're a project manager, use your power of expertise to help the executives in your organization understand the true role and competencies of a great project sponsor. Educating executive management about the skills and competencies of a good project sponsor increases your odds of getting a sponsor who meets your and the project's needs.

There are many ways that you can influence senior executives. The section "Using Your Influence" in Chapter 2 provides detailed guidance for influencing others. It is focused on how you can influence your sponsor, but the tips can be used with other executives as well. Think about which ones will work best in your organizational culture and with your personal communication and influencing style. You can also consider these influencing efforts:

- Write a formal issue paper on the need for stronger sponsorship development within an organization (or *your* organization).

- Arrange to present sponsorship best practices at a future executive meeting.

- Request a one-on-one meeting with an executive who has high interest in and influence on the general project practices within the organization.

- Document the lessons learned from your last project, including action steps, to educate the organization.

- Go out on a limb when you need to. Ask those awkward questions, challenge the other person, or simply ask for help.

Whenever you communicate with executives about sponsorship, you will need to describe the current state, your recommendations, and the likely benefits of the organization's changing its approach toward sponsorship.

WHAT EXECUTIVES CAN DO

An organization's executive managers sanction the projects that they believe will deliver the business' strategic objectives. To succeed in these initiatives, it is logical that they would want these projects to be as low-risk as possible.

Key to reducing risk is the provision of the correct environment for all of the project personnel to thrive and to deliver to the best of their potential capability. All experience and research show a strong and positive correlation between the effectiveness of sponsors and the success of the projects they sponsor; they also show the same regarding project managers' effectiveness and the success of the projects they manage. These two roles need to be equally supported within an organization. Therefore, it logically follows that improving project sponsorship will directly and significantly contribute to improved outcomes for projects the organization performs.

What, if anything, does your organization do for your sponsor community? How do you help sponsors be the best that they can be? If you think there is more you can do to support your sponsors, and you are persuaded by the arguments that there is real value in doing more, then you need to take the next steps in bringing about a shift in sponsor quality. You might wish to take a look at the "Too Cool for School: Making Sponsorship Training Work" section in Chapter 7 to consider the options for developing sponsors, and you may also need to consider taking some external advice on how to make the most effective positive changes to your sponsoring community.

But whatever you do . . . **do something.**

CATEGORIZING PROJECTS AND SELECTING SPONSORS

Many organizations have reached a level of project maturity that allows them to recognize that the projects they initiate fall within different categories. One reason to categorize projects is to understand the impact and potential risk that each kind of project places on the business. The organization can then counter-assess the risks against the expected benefits. This is the first level of project categorization. This exercise is also beneficial in determining the best sponsor for your organization's projects.

Projects are typically profiled using a combination of weights or degrees of importance or impact, according to various aspects or features of each project (Table 7-1). All of these factors can be combined to identify a composite complexity (or risk) category—the "profile" of the project. All projects are not equal, after all, and it is essential to understand each project individually in order to appreciate its risk/benefit ratio for the business.

Aspect	Feature
Commercial	o Type of contract or cost model imposed o Financial impact or penalties that may result o Hierarchy of suppliers (third parties, etc.)
Customer	o Experience in project activity o Previous engagement experience o Appetite for change
Geographic	o Single or multiple locations o Single or multiple countries o Cultural complexity
Deliverables	o Originality of product or outcome o Stability or maturity of input products
Time	o Flexibility of time to deliver o Realism of time constraints o Fixed milestones
Risk profile	Strategic importance

TABLE 7-1: Project Profiling Features

The next level, which many organizations are now moving to, is aligning the selection of some project elements, such as the assignment of the project manager, the determination of which project delivery methodology or framework will be used, and the appointment of the project sponsor, with the way the project is categorized.

Project risk (profile) should also be a key factor in assigning a sponsor: Higher-risk projects will require project sponsors who possess greater influence with stakeholders and greater experience in dealing with complex projects.

If you end up with a complex/high-risk project that is strategically important to the business, you would surely allocate your most experienced project manager and most experienced project sponsor to the job.

Conversely, if it were a small, simple, short-term, single-location, "we have done something like this before" sort of project, a less experienced project manager and project sponsor combination could be used.

It's logical that a company that categorizes its projects and allocates the right project managers to them should take the next logical step: allocating the right—that is, suitably experienced—project sponsor to the role.

CAN YOUR PROJECT MANAGEMENT OFFICE HELP?

Is it possible that in an organization with weak or limited project sponsor capability, the project management office (PMO) could act as a sponsor for smaller projects? It is surely better to do this rather than not use sponsors at all. If a particular project is in direct support of the organization's project practices (e.g., implementing Microsoft Project Server), then the PMO will make a good sponsor.

The PMO also might be a politically acceptable body to provide discrete support for project sponsors should it be required (and if, of course, the project sponsors acknowledge they need help). Because the PMO is the governing body for the organization's project methodology and standards, it is natural that its duties would also include sponsorship tasks and deliverables. The PMO could easily and sensitively provide coaching and advice upon request.

It could also be the PMO's role to garner and disseminate lessons learned to the project community, including issues with sponsorship capability.

Think about which of the key sponsorship activities might be suitable for a PMO to offer, as some form of interim resource. Which ones might a PMO not be able to offer in any effective way?

A PMO may support the board by

- **Offering leadership for the project.** This is possible as long as the PMO representative can operate in some form of objective silo from the rest of the PMO's project activity.

- **Owning the business case.** The PMO needs additional support, in part from a senior executive, to gain the right level of knowledge and independence from the business.

- **Ensuring the project is aligned to the business strategy.** This could be done as long as the PMO operates at the right level in the organization (i.e., one that is aligned to and involved in the strategic planning activities) and is up-to-date with regard to the organization's current strategic intention and thought.

- **Governing the risk of the project.** The PMO should easily be able to do this.

- **Engaging and communicating with all stakeholders.** This should be achievable as long as the PMO sits at the right level to interact with all stakeholders appropriately.

- **Owning the realization of benefits.** This is a challenging one. If the PMO is focused on project success and the mechanics of project delivery and project management development, and more, this may be a step too far for the PMO.

- **Offering assurance of success.** The PMO can offer some degree of success assurance, but sometimes the executive may need to provide high-level assistance.

- **Arbitrating as required for the good of the business.** This is difficult if the arbitration involves management levels above that of the PMO's management.

- **Overseeing the process of incorporating lessons learned back into the business.** The PMO can and should play a key role here.

A PMO may support the project manager by

- **Being a decisionmaker.** The PMO can make decisions about project management support if the business grants it the authority to do so.

- **Clarifying issues as required.** The PMO must be in the know about the issue at hand to make clarifications.

- **Resolving business issues that impact the project.** It's unlikely that a PMO, however high up in the business, will be able to do this without additional executive support.

- **Managing high-level relationships.** The PMO can manage such relationships to a degree, as long as its management is mature and experienced. But there may be situations in which there is a need for high-level intervention from the executive.

- **Helping with resourcing challenges.** The PMO can assist with resourcing needs but will no doubt have to call upon the goodwill of business managers. Also, situations could arise in which there are major conflicts in resource prioritization and a top-level decision is required.

- **Supporting the project manager.** This is a natural role for the PMO, as it is the de facto community of practice for the project managers of the organization (e.g., looking after their training, skill development, and certification).

- **Applying objective comment and guidance.** Though this is generally possible, there could be moments of internal conflict when the overall ownership of the PMO's portfolio of projects has to be considered over and above that of any individual project (or project manager).

A PMO may support the project team by

- **Offering leadership of purpose.** The PMO can provide such leadership if project team members hold it in high regard.
- **Offering authority and representation of the business.** The PMO will need to be backed by some senior executive or management body.
- **Championing the project and helping the team understand the project's benefits to the organization.** The actual business side of the project should do this.

We can see that even the best-intentioned PMO cannot offer everything that a sponsor should provide, but there is still a very strong argument that, in the absence of a project sponsor, the PMO can fill a void. In this case, something is definitely better than nothing.

NOTES

1. We hope that this book will at least contribute to sponsors' gaining insight into what they should be doing (if they aren't doing it already) and how to go about developing their skills.
2. The Standish Group, *Chaos Manifesto 2012: The Year of the Executive Sponsor* (Boston: The Standish Group, 2012), 64.
3. The Standish Group, *Chaos Manifesto 2012: The Year of the Executive Sponsor* (Boston: The Standish Group, 2012), 49.
4. Ibid.
5. Ibid.

When it comes to the future, there are three kinds of people: those who let it happen, those who make it happen, and those who wonder what happened.

—John M. Richardson

Afterword

In our experience, the skill profile of project managers continues to grow, and more and more organizations are developing project managers in a disciplined and mature manner. The days of the accidental project manager are mostly long gone. But the same cannot be said of all project sponsors. Many still wrongly believe that the project sponsor is just a figurehead who is never called to active duty.

How wrong. How *very* wrong.

We carried out a literature search on the topic of project sponsorship (see Appendix E) and found both a lack of information and guidance for project sponsors and a general failure to recognize the key role of the sponsor. From personal experience gained through working in many organizations around the world, we have come across extremely few examples of businesses that have any form of sponsorship support or development. This is further substantiated by the feedback we received through the survey undertaken for this book: 74 percent of respondents stated that there was nothing in place to help sponsors inside their organizations (see Appendix A).

We would like to officially launch the "Campaign for Real Project Sponsors," an effort that urges organizations to make a real investment in anyone who acts in such a key role. **Please join the campaign** by proactively providing information to your organization and sponsors on best practices in project governance. Doing so would help build a great future for project sponsors, project managers, and projects in general. You can join the campaign by visiting our website (at www.strategies4sponsors.com) to share in the exchange of ideas and best practices.

We'd particularly like to see investment in the education of all managers, executives, and leaders. Every manager who reaches a certain level in his career is likely to be called upon to sponsor a project, so sponsorship training should be part of the standard curriculum in all business classes. This would begin to provide a good foundation for sponsors and project managers to begin their professional relationship as they will have a common understanding of project-based activity and the roles and responsibilities each has to adhere to.

So how can you contribute to our campaign?

- Read this book. (I guess you can tick this one off!)
- Spread the word amongst your peers about this book and the campaign.
- Join the Project Sponsors group on LinkedIn.
- Start or join in discussions about project sponsorship on other relevant LinkedIn groups.
- Mention it in discussions with your project management teams.
- Talk about it during meetings of your local project management chapter or other professional organization.
- Blog about it and/or contribute to blogs on the subject. (Notify us at strategies4sponsors.com so we can cross-promote your post.)
- Podcast about it.

- Tweet about it.
- Post on Facebook about it.
- Thank your sponsor today for all of his good work.

Data is not information, information is not knowledge, knowledge is not understanding, understanding is not wisdom.

—Clifford Stoll

APPENDIX A
Sponsorship Survey Results

As part of the research for this book, we carried out a survey to learn more about people's experiences with project sponsorship in the real world. This appendix covers the key points of the feedback from this survey along with an additional survey question conducted by Project Agency, Ron Rosenhead's training company. Survey results are provided as a courtesy to those who participated and should readers wish to delve a little deeper into the feedback we received.

THE STRATEGIES FOR PROJECT SPONSORSHIP SURVEY

The survey, conducted in early 2012, received more than 200 responses. Figure A-1 shows respondents' roles.

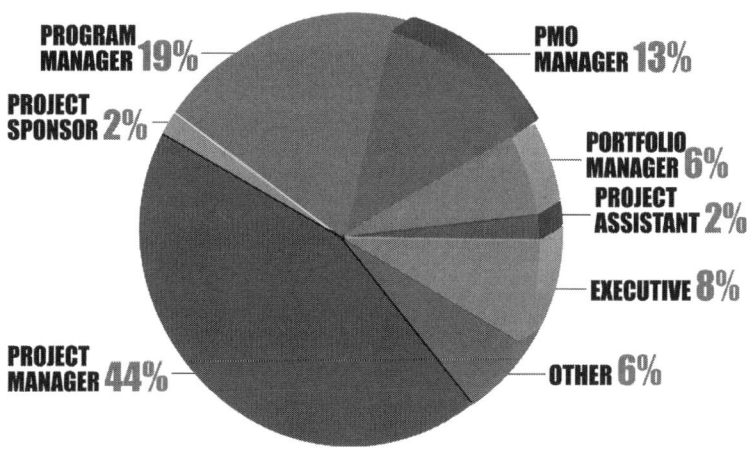

FIGURE A-1: Primary Roles on Projects

It was important to gain insight from people in a broad range of roles and, in general, we achieved this, although few respondents considered themselves primarily to be project sponsors. Assuming that those who described themselves as executives have some sponsoring responsibilities, ten percent of the responses came from people we can include in the sponsor community. We also know from the plentiful feedback we received that a number of senior project personnel also act in a sponsor role.

Figure A-2 shows that, in general, the respondents were experienced in project management. More than 85 percent of respondents had more than five years of experience, and 63 percent had more than ten years' experience. Only one percent are what we might consider "newbies."

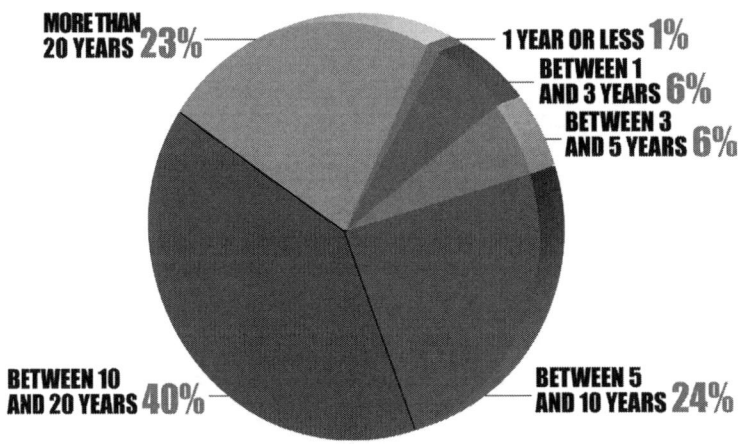

FIGURE A-2: Tenure in Project Management

We then asked what project-supporting activities organizations had in place. As shown in Figure A-3, most had what might currently be considered essential initiatives. The majority of organizations had program management offices (PMOs), some form of lessons-learned process, a project management methodology or framework, a project approval process, and training programs. The only listed activity that was relatively rare was a certification policy.

Obviously, having some of these elements in place and using them wisely and efficiently, or even using them at all, are two different things. A number of comments from respondents pointed to two disturbing themes:

- A lessons-learned process is often conducted and the lessons documented, but they are never used in planning subsequent projects.

- Processes are identified but rarely followed, indicating weak governance.

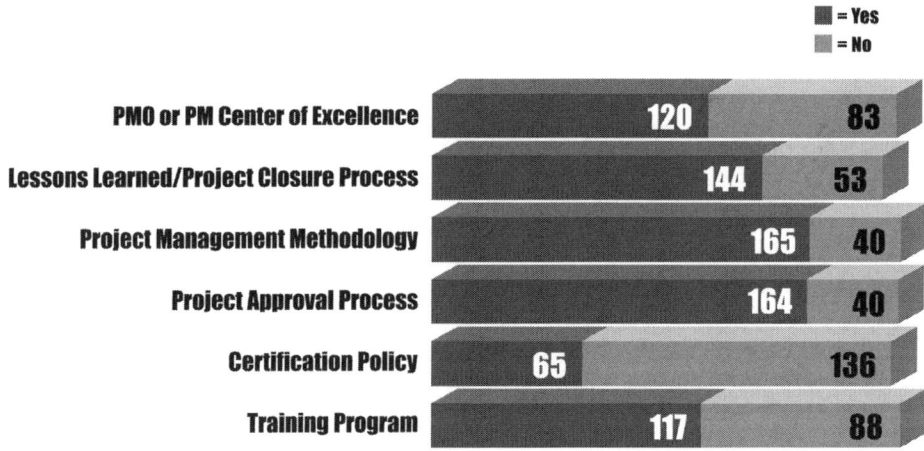

FIGURE A-3: Project-Supporting Activities

One respondent pointed to a lack of consistency, saying that sponsors and project managers themselves determine what methodologies are used, which creates problems. Projects are handled very differently across the organization, based on the personal preferences of the project manager or sponsor involved, meaning subject matter experts, end users, executive management, and others who work on multiple projects are constantly being confronted with different methodologies, leading to confusion and longer turnaround times.

It seems there is definitely room for improvement.

Figure A-4 shows that only 14 percent of organizations do not at least recognize the role of project sponsor. But even among the 85 percent that do, there were some worrying comments, such as, "The sponsor does not know he is the sponsor. If he knows, he does not understand his duties. And if occasionally he knows he is the sponsor and understands his role, his decisions get overruled by business managers or directors."

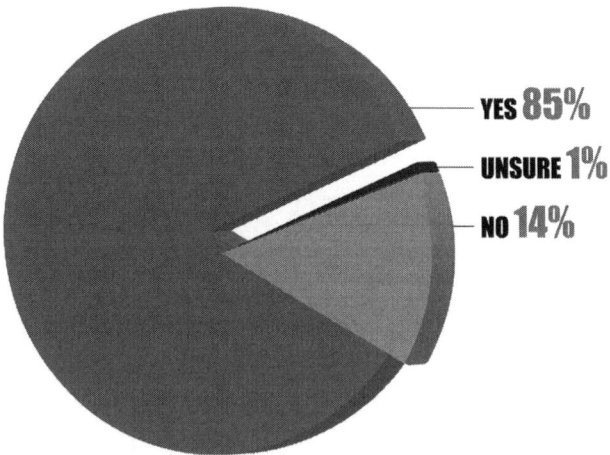

FIGURE A-4: Use of Project Sponsors

So it seems it is not all rosy in the world of project sponsorship. But what can organizations do to develop good sponsorship and to help sponsors understand their duties and represent both the business and the project effectively? Figure A-5 illustrates the prevalence of sponsor training.

Some respondents—17 percent—indicated that sponsors in their organizations did receive some training, but a concerning 74 percent said that sponsors are not offered such support. When sponsor training does exist, its quality and depth are often questionable. Most of the training the survey participants mentioned occurred during project briefings or short-duration models and simply was not comprehensive.

Participants' comments suggested that many sponsors do not understand their role; but they also indicated that in many cases, sponsors believe that they do not need training, guidance, advice, support, or even just a good book on the subject, even when the organization offers it.

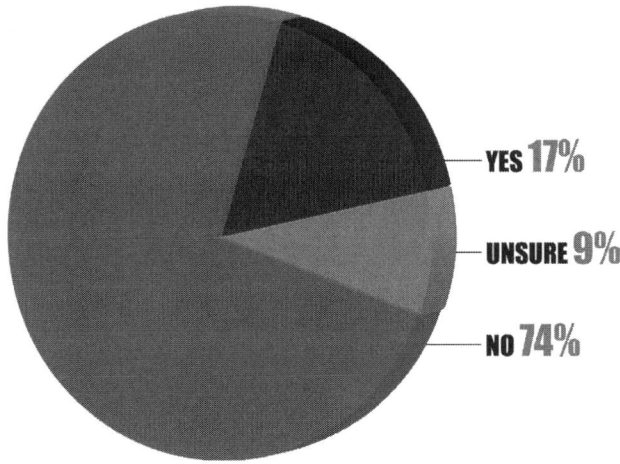

FIGURE A-5: Prevalence of Sponsor Training

What about the impact sponsors, trained or otherwise, have on organizations? Figure A-6 shows that 79 percent of respondents felt that having a sponsor in place has at least some positive effects on project success, but five percent saw sponsorship as having a negative impact. Only 34 percent said that sponsors have a very good impact on success.

Respondents seemed to agree that the project sponsor can make or break the project: *Projects will not be successful without a supportive and active sponsor in place.*

The true test for project sponsorship is when the going gets tough. Bad sponsors will conveniently focus on "other priorities" when a project is challenged. Great sponsors will get involved, bringing support, perspective, and credibility—making it more likely that the project will succeed.

Without the right sponsor, we find, the project is doomed before it starts.

An engaged sponsor often adds great value to the project if she can keep her eye on the business case instead of the project work details.

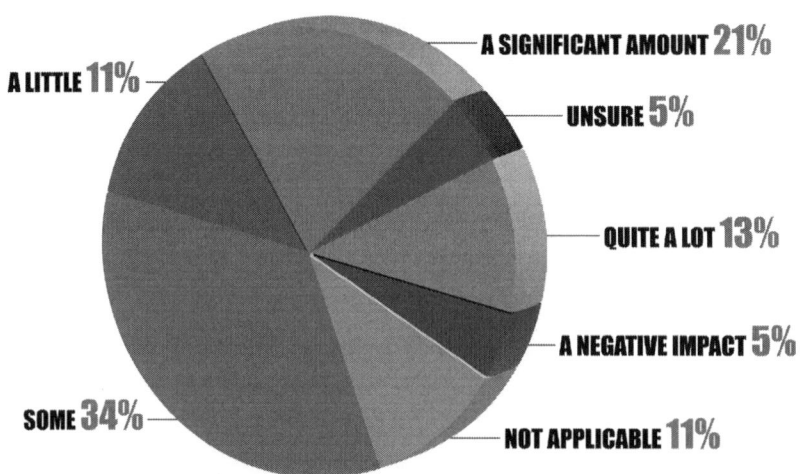

FIGURE A-6: Impact of Sponsors on Project Success

It seemed as if people were questioning their own project experience and the effectiveness of specific sponsors rather than the concept of project sponsorship itself. When asked about *good* project sponsorship, the overwhelming majority indicated the role is important.

As shown in Figure A-7, an overwhelming 99.5 percent of respondents think that having a good project sponsor is important or even critical to project success, which validates the mere existence of the role within the project structure.

So it seems that sponsorship is a key role, but survey participants have had mixed experiences in working with or working as a project sponsor.

Participants said that the reasons good project sponsorship is important include removing barriers, providing leadership, keeping the big picture in mind, and championing the project. One asked, "If a project is not adequately sponsored and owned by the business, why do it?"

Good question.

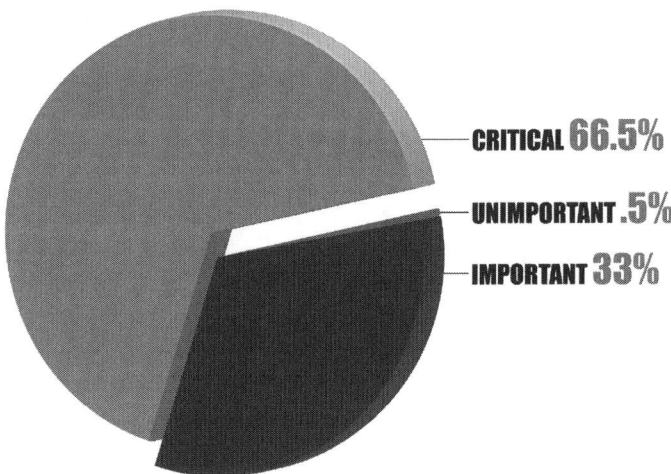

FIGURE A-7: Importance of a Good Sponsor

Apart from training, we wondered about participants' experiences with other sources of knowledge and information on sponsorship. We asked about reading material on the subject. Figure A-8 shows that only 13 percent of respondents have read a "good" book on project sponsorship.[1]

Among the participants who named specific resources, five respondents listed *Project Sponsorship: Achieving Management Commitment for Project Success* by Randy Englund and Alfonso Bucero, two people mentioned books on PRINCE2, and a few people recommended books by David West, Peter Taylor, and Peter Drucker.[2] Participants also suggested many leadership books, too.

What about other resources? The website projectmanagement.com (formerly gantthead.com)[3] was the most frequently mentioned; also noted were the Harvard Business School's website, PMChat,[4] Gartner,[5] LinkedIn groups,[6] and GAPPS.[7]

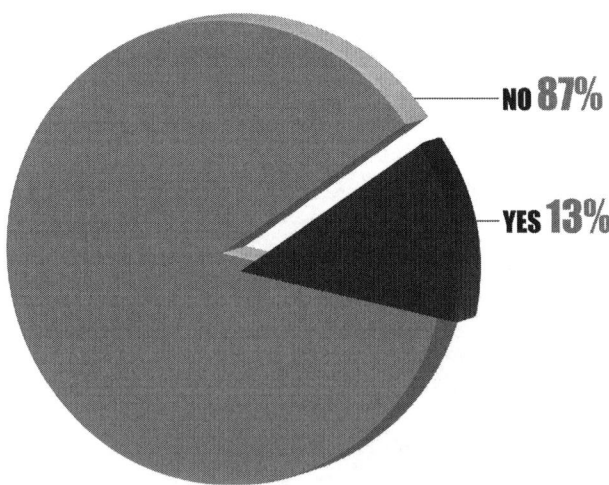

FIGURE A-8: Frequency of Reading Good Books on Sponsorship

We then asked participants if they wanted to be a project sponsor. Less than ten percent indicated that they would not consider taking a sponsor role in the future; 25 percent were unsure or thought the question was not applicable. That leaves 65 percent thinking about sponsorship as a future role or responsibility. We hope that these people will become non-accidental project sponsors.

Those who said they would consider becoming sponsors spoke of feeling well prepared for the role based on their project experience. Only a handful of respondents indicated that their interest would be contingent on their level of influence and authority in the organization.

PROJECT AGENCY'S RESEARCH

If it's true that project management has matured in the 30 years since the title *project sponsor* came into being, and that companies are now recognizing the real value that project management can bring to the bottom line and how it can contribute to delivery of their strategy, companies should then have a clear understanding of the role project sponsorship plays, too. But do they?

Another survey,[8] involving almost 1,500 people who completed it before taking a project management course between 2002 and 2012, can help us answer that question. Participants were asked whether they agreed with the statement "There is always clear sponsorship defined for our projects."

Figure A-9 shows that only 39 percent thought that the sponsor's role was clearly defined for their projects. A much larger percentage—nearly half—felt otherwise.

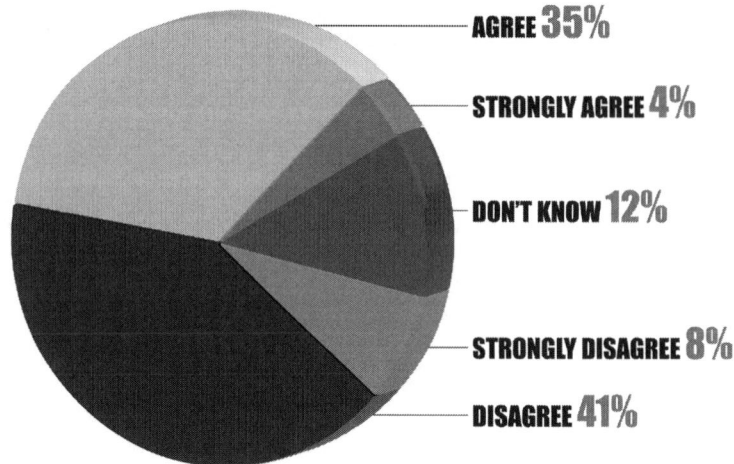

FIGURE A-9: Definition of the Sponsor's Role

Evidently, companies do not have a clear understanding of the role the sponsor plays. If they did, the responses we gathered in our own research would be much more positive and consistent.

While project management may have matured, the role of the project sponsor has not. As our survey indicates, the vast majority of respondents' projects have sponsors, and nearly everyone surveyed indicated that the sponsor's role is important or critical to their projects, but if sponsorship is not clearly defined, more risks are sure to arise for the project and project manager.

Effort and energy have been put into training project managers, but not enough has been done to train those who sit in the sponsor chair. (Recall that according to our survey, only 17 percent of sponsors have received some form of training for the role.) One barrier is sponsors' interest and availability. Only seven percent of survey respondents indicated that project sponsor is a full-time position in their organization. It is easy to see why it would be difficult for a project sponsor to make time to pursue training, given the competing interests he must juggle.

We also learned from our survey that many project sponsors do not believe that they need training. They are experts in their field of business, but it is not easy for them to recognize the additional skills and best practices that will increase the chances of project success. We as project managers can leverage a project sponsor's pride in his work and success to help make him a better sponsor. We have come to realize that progress in this area will largely depend on project managers developing skills in "managing up" the organization. That means helping project sponsors understand their roles and what is needed from them.[9]

NOTES

1. Obviously, our goal is for 100 percent of readers of this book to answer this question in the affirmative!
2. Additional books are listed in Appendix E.
3. Online community for IT project managers that offers resources and expertise in a variety of topics.
4. Project Management Chat is a weekly Twitter chat hosted by Robert Kelly and Rob Prinzo each Friday from 12:00–1:00 p.m. (EST) via hashtag #PMChat.
5. Gartner is the world's leading information technology research and advisory company.
6. LinkedIn is a social networking website for people in professional occupations. As of February 2012, LinkedIn reported more than 150 million registered users in more than 200 countries and territories. LinkedIn promotes communities of interest, known as *groups,* as part of its networking capability. We started a group called *Project Sponsors,* which hundreds of LinkedIn users have joined. Mature, ongoing discussions have come out of the group.
7. The Global Alliance for Project Performance Standards, or GAPPS, "is a unique alliance of government, private industry, professional associations, and training/academic institutes working together to develop globally applicable project management competency based standards, frameworks, and mappings." (From the GAPPS official website, "About Us," http://www.globalpmstandards.org/main/page_about_us.html.)
8. Project Agency carried out this research among attendees of its project management courses.
9. Randall L. Englund and Alfonso Bucero, *The Complete Project Manager: Integrating People, Organizational, and Technical Skills* (Tysons Corner, VA: Management Concepts, 2012).

APPENDIX B
The Definitive Project Sponsor Checklist

We developed, through a literature search, discussions with fellow professionals in the project management world, and their experience, a definitive list of activities that we believe the sponsor should undertake. The list below is referenced several times throughout the book or presented in modified form and is provided here as a standalone document for easier reference and sharing.

1	Provides direction and guidance for strategies and initiatives
2	Works with the project manager to develop the project charter
3	Identifies and quantifies business benefits to be achieved by successful implementation of the project
4	Makes go/no-go decisions
5	Evaluates the project's success upon completion
6	Negotiates funding for the project
7	Actively participates in the initial project planning
8	Reviews and approves changes to plans, priorities, deliverables, schedule, and more
9	Identifies project steering committee members
10	Gains agreement among stakeholders when differences of opinion occur
11	Chairs the project steering committee
12	Assists the project when required (especially in an out-of-control situation) by exerting organizational authority and the ability to influence
13	Helps resolve interproject boundary issues
14	Supports the project manager in conflict resolution
15	Advises the project manager of protocols, political issues, and potential sensitivities
16	Makes the project visible within the organization
17	Encourages stakeholder involvement and builds and maintains their ongoing commitment through effective communication strategies

APPENDIX C
The Definitive Project Manager Checklist

Fully briefs project sponsors, stakeholders, and, if appropriate, the project team
Coaches and advises the project sponsor of project needs
Proactively monitors and reports delivery of project against key deliverables
Is ultimately accountable for the project processes and team
Provides adequate background, analysis, and recommendations to support needed decisions
Where appropriate, staffs the steering committee (project board); arranges for the committee's administrative needs to be met directly or through delegation
Provides timely and sufficient information about potential resource needs
Fully understands the organization's strategy and how projects fit into it
Provides project documentation that informs the sponsor and stakeholders of project plans and status
Monitors and tracks the change management process, bringing necessary items to the project sponsor's or steering committee's (project board's) attention
Keeps the sponsor informed on budget and schedule tracking; alerts her early of potential shortfalls and offers recommendations to respond or adjust
Understands project status at all times and how it fits with the organization's project status as well as the overall project management approach used internally.
Demonstrates strong leadership throughout the project
Promotes partnership/collaborative working across the organization and externally
Networks effectively and brokers good relationships with stakeholders
Is able to demonstrate effective communication in all areas
Fully understands project management and its implications for project success
Fully understands the project management life cycle model and can guide others in its use
Responds to notice of protocols, political issues, and potential sensitivities by actively tracking risks (including mitigation and contingency strategies) and issues
Provides information to the sponsor on project barriers with context, background, and recommended actions

APPENDIX D
The 50 Secrets to Being a Good Executive Sponsor[1]

- Secret 1: Inspire
- Secret 2: Know How the Solution Will Be Used
- Secret 3: Understand the Project Management Process
- Secret 4: Set Goals
- Secret 5: Get the Right Project Resources
- Secret 6: Promote Excellence
- Secret 7: Understand Business Events
- Secret 8: Communicate the Facts
- Secret 9: Reward Outstanding Effort
- Secret 10: Provide Clarity of Purpose
- Secret 11: Recognize Team Member Contributions
- Secret 12: Obtain Decision Acceptance
- Secret 13: Develop Quality User Relationships
- Secret 14: Understand the Executive Sponsor Role
- Secret 15: Understand Risk and Reward

- Secret 16: Make Quick Decisions
- Secret 17: Demand Objectivity and Transparency
- Secret 18: Manage Financial Changes
- Secret 19: Determine Explicit User Needs
- Secret 20: Endorse the Business Objectives
- Secret 21: Distribute Decision Power
- Secret 22: Overcome Arrogance
- Secret 23: Overcome Fraudulence
- Secret 24: Use Value and Risk Metrics
- Secret 25: Understand the Project Life Cycle
- Secret 26: Understand Project Management Techniques
- Secret 27: Overcome Ignorance
- Secret 28: Have a Succinct Vision
- Secret 29: Know When to Pull the Plug
- Secret 30: Develop a Simple Vision
- Secret 31: Track Progress with Metrics
- Secret 32: Drive Project Activities
- Secret 33: Celebrate Accomplishments
- Secret 34: Track Investments
- Secret 35: Track Technical Events
- Secret 36: Have Commitment

- Secret 37: Be Familiar with Similar Projects
- Secret 38: Overcome Overambition
- Secret 39: Establish a Common Vocabulary
- Secret 40: Use a Decision Pipeline
- Secret 41: Deliver Steppingstones
- Secret 42: Track Progress Against the Plan
- Secret 43: Create a Community
- Secret 44: Exhibit Honor and Pride
- Secret 45: Overcome Abstinence
- Secret 46: Avoid Decision Latency
- Secret 47: Negotiate
- Secret 48: Be Aware
- Secret 49: Bond with the Project Manager
- Secret 50: Celebrate with a Party

NOTES

1. The Standish Group, *Chaos Manifesto 2012: The Year of the Executive Sponsor* (Boston: The Standish Group, 2012), 3.

APPENDIX E
Additional Resources on Project Sponsorship

There are a number of interesting books on project sponsorship that you might like to read after this one.

Association for Project Management. *Sponsoring Change: A Guide to the Governance Aspects of Project Sponsorship*. Princes Risborough, Buckinghamshire, UK: Association for Project Management, 2009.

Crawford, Lynn, Terry Cooke-Davies, and Brian Hobbs. *Situational Sponsorship of Projects and Programs: An Empirical Review*. Newtown Square, PA: Project Management Institute, 2008.

Englund, Randall L., and Alfonso Bucero. *Project Sponsorship: Achieving Management Commitment for Project Success*. San Francisco: Jossey-Bass, 2006.

Love, Neil, and Joan Brandt-Love. *The Project Sponsor Guide*. Newtown Square, PA: Project Management Institute, 2000.

West, David. *Project Sponsorship: An Essential Guide for Those Sponsoring Projects Within Their Organizations*. Farnham, Surrey, UK: Gower, 2010.

We suggest the following online resources as well:

Alessandri, Marie-Dominique, Kristell Le Garrec, and Edward Popelard. *Exploring the Role of the Project Sponsor.* Master's thesis, ESC Lille, 2003–2005; http://www.devesc.fr/mediadoc/20060199.pdf.

James, Vicki, Ron Rosenhead, and Peter Taylor. Strategies for Project Sponsorship; www.strategies4sponsors.com.

PM Podcast. "Episode 193: The GAPPS Standard for Project Sponsors" [podcast]; http://www.project-management-podcast.com/index.php/podcast-episodes/episode-details/406-episode-193-the-gapps-standard-for-project-sponsors.

Index

A

absent sponsors
    case notes 1, 76
    case notes 2, 77–79
    change request example, 67–69
    prescription, 75
    prognosis, 75
    symptoms, 75
accidental project sponsors, 123–124
allegiance approach, influence, 51
APM. *See* Association for Project Management
arbitration, 166
asking sponsors for help, 52–53
assessing sponsors, 19
Association for Project Management (APM), 9
assurance of success, 165
authority, 167

B

bad news, delivering, 57–59
bad sponsors
    case notes 1, 95–96
    case notes 2, 96
    case notes 3, 96–97
    case notes 4, 97
    impact, 8
    prescription, 95
    prognosis, 95
    symptoms, 94
balanced sponsorship competency framework, 157–159
budget constraints, 133
bureaucratic power, 23
business benefits, 133
business benefits, identifying and quantifying, 133–135
business problem statement, 133
business strategy, aligning project with, 165
busy sponsors, 79–81

C

categorizing projects, 162–164
Celebrate Accomplishments (Standish Group Secret 33), 158
CFO. *See* chief financial officer
challenging sponsors
    absent, 75–79
    busy, 79–81
    committees, 91–94
    inexperienced, 83–84

overview, 73–74
problem, 97–99
saboteur, 94–97
sponsor who gets involved too late, 87–89
sponsor who wants to be project manager, 84–87
uninterested, 81–83
untrained, 89–91
championing projects, 167
change request for missing sponsor, 67–69
changes, reviewing, 139–140
charismatic power, 24
chief financial officer (CFO), 109
chief information officer (CIO), 76–78, 120
choosing sponsors, 17–18
clarifying issues, 166
coaching, 60–61
coercive power, 23
commercial aspect of projects, 163
committee of sponsors
    case notes, 92–94
    prescription, 92
    prognosis, 91
    symptoms, 91
communications planning
    benefits, 41
    goals, 41
    overview, 39–40
    project manager responsibilities, 42–44
    questions, 41–42
    sample plan, 42–43
    survey results, 40
conflict resolution, 142

consulting approach, influence, 50
Create a Community (Standish Group Secret 43), 158
customer aspect of projects, 163
customer relationship management (CRM), 135

D

decision-making process, 37–38
decisionmakers, 166
deliverables, 163
Demand Objectivity and Transparency (Standish Group Secret 17), 158
Deming cycle, 59–60
determining sponsor's interests, 35
direct influence, 49
discussion topics for sponsor, 33–34
duties, project managers and sponsors, 11

E

emergencies, 53
exchange approach, influence, 50–51
executing projects, 11

F

feedback, providing to sponsor
    guidelines, 53–54
    importance, 53
    making recommendations, 56–57
    rules, 55–56
    sample dialogue, 54–55
Fifty Secrets, The Standish Group, 153–159

financial power, 23
first meeting with sponsor, 30–33
friendship approach, influence, 50
funding, negotiating, 138–139

G

geographic aspect of projects, 163
go/no-go decisions, 135–136
good cop, bad cop, 24
good sponsors, 6–7
guidance strategies and initiatives, 132
A Guide to the Project Management Body of Knowledge (PMBOK Guide), 3

H

Have Commitment (Standish Group Secret 36), 158
help, asking sponsor for, 52–53
high-level relationships, 166
high-level risks, 133
human resources (HR), 110, 149

I

inexperienced sponsors
   case notes, 84
   prescription, 83
   prognosis, 83
   symptoms, 83
influence
   allegiance approach, 51
   consulting approach, 50
   direct, 49
   exchange approach, 50–51
   friendship approach, 50
   legitimacy approach, 49
   logic approach, 51
   modeling approach, 52
   persuasion, 50–51
   request approach, 49
   social, 51–52
   social approach, 51
   through appeal, 49–50
   types, 48–49
   value approach, 49–50
influence map
   creating, 112–114
   definition, 108
   elements, 109
   example, 109–112
initiating projects, 11
Inspire (Standish Group Secret 1), 158
interproject boundary issues, 142
interviewing sponsor candidates
   evaluating, 29–30
   examples, 27–28
   importance, 25
   questions, 26
involved, balanced sponsor competency framework, 158–159

K

keep informed, power grid, 21–22
keep satisfied, power grid, 21
Know How the Solution Will be Used (Standish Group Secret 2), 158

L

leadership of purpose, 167
legitimacy approach, influence, 49
legitimate power, 23
lessons learned, 166

logic approach, influence, 51
loss of sponsor, 67–69

M

Make Quick Decisions (Standish Group Secret 16), 158
manage closely, power grid, 21
managing high-level relationships, 166
managing relationship with sponsor, 19–21
modeling approach, influence, 52
monitor, power grid, 22
monitoring and controlling projects, 11

N

negotiating funding, 138–139
now and wow factor, 99–102

O

objective, balanced sponsor competency framework, 158–159
objective comments and guidance, 167
Obtain Decision Acceptance (Standish Group Secret 12), 158
offering leadership, 165
open discussions, 35–36
organizational strategy and objectives, 133
out of control, defining, 141
owning the business case, 165

P

persuasion, 50–51
plan-do-check-act cycle, 59
planning projects, 11
PMBOK Guide. *See A Guide to the Project Management Body of Knowledge*
PMI. *See* Project Management Institute
PMO. *See* project management office
political issues, 144
power
    bureaucratic, 23
    charismatic, 24
    coercive, 23
    financial, 23
    good cop, bad cop, 24
    legitimate, 23
    project manager, 25
    project sponsor, 24–25
    referent, 24
    reward, 23
    technical, 24
    types of, 22
power grid, 19–21
PRINCE2, 10
problem sponsors, 97–99
project boards, 140
project charters, 133
project closure, 11
project failure, 7
project governance structure, 133
Project Management Institute (PMI), 3
project management office (PMO), 79, 151, 164–167
project manager evaluation tool, 69–71

project manager responsibilities,
  communications planning,
  42–44
project managers
  assessing sponsors, 19
  choosing sponsors, 17–18
  determining sponsor's interests,
    35
  discussion topics for sponsor,
    33–34
  duties, 11
  first meeting, 30–33
  power, 25
  power grid, 19–21
  questions for sponsor, 34–35
  relationship with sponsor, 30
  role, 9
  sponsor criteria, 18–19
  transitioning to sponsors,
    124–126
project owner, 9
project passion, sharing with
  sponsor, 66–67
project planning, active
  participation in, 139
project profiling features, 162–163
project risk, 163
project steering committee,
  chairing, 141
project success, 134, 137
project visibility, 142–143
Provide Clarity of Purpose
  (Standish Group Secret 10), 158
providing project assistance, 141

Q

questions for sponsor, 34–35

R

reactive, balanced sponsor
  competency framework,
  158–159
realization of benefits, 165
recommendations, 56–57
referent power, 24
relationship with sponsor, 30
request approach, influence, 49
resolving business issues, 166
resourcing challenges, 166
Reward Outstanding Effort
  (Standish Group Secret 9), 158
reward power, 23
rewarding outstanding effort,
  153, 155–156
risk, 163, 165

S

saboteur sponsors, 94–97
saboteurs
  case notes 1, 95–96
  case notes 2, 96
  case notes 3, 96–97
  case notes 4, 97
  impact, 8
  prescription, 95
  prognosis, 95
  symptoms, 94
schedule constraints, 133
scope constraints, 133
sensitivities, 144
social influence, 51–52
sponsor responsibilities evaluation
  tool
  checklists, evolution of, 61–63
  example, 64–65
  importance, 61

ratings, 65–66
weak sponsorship, 63
sponsors
    acting as project managers, 84–87
    criteria, 18–19
    duties, 11
    expectations, 36
    expectations regarding project managers, 48
    late involvement in project, 87–89
    power, 24–25
    project responsibilities, 126–129
    role of, 5–8
    survey, 119–123
    training, 149–153
sponsorship
    definition, 2–4, 9–10
    developing capability, 160–161
    process, 5
stakeholders
    analysis, 104–107
    encouraging involvement, 143–144
    engagement, 107–108
    identification of, 104
    importance, 103
    matrix, 105
steering committee members, 140
success, 134, 137
sunk cost, 136
supportive, balanced sponsor competency framework, 158–159

T

team support, 38–39
technical power, 24
time aspect of projects, 163
time commitments, 37
tracking progress against plan, 154, 156–157
transitioning from project manager to sponsor, 124–126
types, 48–49

U

Understand Business Events (Standish Group Secret 7), 158
Understand the Project Management Process (Standish Group Secret 3), 158
understanding project management, 153–154
uninterested sponsors, 81–83
untrained sponsors
    case notes, 90–91
    prescription, 89–90
    prognosis, 89
    symptoms, 89

V

value approach, influence, 49–50

Complement Your Project Management Library with These Additional Resources from
MANAGEMENTCONCEPTS PRESS

Maximizing Project Value: A Project Manager's Guide
John Goodpasture

Maximizing project value is about optimizing the tradeoff between project value and business value, two values that are constantly in tension between the project manager and the project sponsor. In this book the author brings his wealth of experience in project management to demonstrate how to increase a project's value and ultimately contribute to the attainment of business goals

ISBN 978-1-56726-393-0 ■ Product Code B930 ■ 300 pages

Practical Project Risk Management: The ATOM Methodology, Second Edition
David Hillson and Peter Simon

Get the "how" of correctly managing project risk in this latest edition of *Practical Project Risk Management: The ATOM Methodology*. The authors, David Hillson and Peter Simon, have applied their extensive experience in managing risk on projects to develop this simple and scalable approach—the ATOM methodology. ATOM—Active Threat and Opportunity Management—is a proven practical approach that all project managers, as well as all members of the project team, can readily understand and use.

ISBN 978-1-56726-366-4 ■ Product Code B664 ■ 258 pages

The Complete Project Manager: Integrating People, Organizational, and Technical Skills
Randall Englund and Alfonso Bucero

This book integrates theory and application, humor and passion, and concepts and examples drawn from the authors' experiences as well as from contributors who share their stories. The concepts are easy to understand, universal, powerful, and readily applicable. There is no complicated model to understand before practicing what you learn…or wish you had learned when starting your career.

ISBN 978-1-56726-359-6 ■ Product Code B596 ■ 284 pages

The Complete Project Manager's Toolkit
Randall Englund and Alfonso Bucero

The Complete Project Manager's Toolkit will enable you to implement the easy-to-understand, universal, powerful, and immediately applicable concepts presented in *The Complete Project Manager*. You may already be aware of *what* you need to do; this book supplies the *how*.

Although *The Complete Project Manager's Toolkit* alone book, it is designed to complement *The Complete Project Manager: Integrating People, Organizational, and Technical Skills*.

ISBN 978-1-56726-360-2 ■ Product Code B602 ■ 203 pages

The Project Management Essential Library

The Project Management Essential Library is a series of eleven books, each of which covers a separate and distinct area of project management. The series provides project managers with new skills, clear explanations, and innovative approaches to the fundamentals of managing projects effectively. Whether further developing the skills you already have or adding tools to your repertoire, you will find insights in *The Project Management Essential Library* that you can immediately implement.

The Project Management Essential Library
Choose individual volumes ... or the complete library ...
And give your projects the best chance of success!

Six Sigma for Project Managers
Steve Neuendorf
ISBN 978-1-56726-146-2
Product Code B469

Project Estimating and Cost Management
Parviz F. Rad, PhD, PMP
ISBN 978-1-56726-144-8 ■ Product Code B442

The Triple Constraints in Project Management
Michael S. Dobson, PMP
ISBN 978-1-56726-152-3
Product Code B523

Effective Work Breakdown Structures
Gregory T. Haugan, PhD, PMP
ISBN 978-1-56726-135-6 ■ Product Code B353

Project Leadership
Timothy J. Kloppenborg, PhD, PMP, Arthur Shriberg, EdD, and Jayashree Venkatraman
ISBN 978-1-56726-145-5 ■ Product Code B450

Project Planning and Scheduling
Gregory T. Haugan, PhD, PMP
ISBN 978-1-56726-136-3 ■ Product Code B361

Managing Projects for Value
John C. Goodpasture, PMP
ISBN 978-1-56726-138-8 ■ Product Code B388

Managing Project Quality
Timothy J. Kloppenborg, PhD, PMP, and Joseph A. Petrick, PhD
ISBN 978-1-56726-141-7 ■ Product Code B418

Project Risk Management: A Proactive Approach
Paul S. Royer, PMP
ISBN 978-1-56726-139-4 ■ Product Code B396

Managing Project Integration
Denis F. Cioffi, PhD
ISBN 978-1-56726-134-9 ■ Product Code B345

Project Measurement
Steve Neuendorf
ISBN 978-1-56726-140-0 ■ Product Code B40X

Full Set
Product Code B54X

Order today for a 30-day risk-free trial!
Visit www.managementconcepts.com/pubs or call 703-790-9595